Library of
Davidson College

THE SYRIAN-AFRICAN RIFT
AND OTHER POEMS

JEWISH POETRY SERIES
Allen Mandelbaum / Yehuda Amichai   GENERAL EDITORS

Pamela White Hadas
IN LIGHT OF GENESIS

Else Lasker-Schüler
HEBREW BALLADS AND OTHER POEMS

Avoth Yeshurun
THE SYRIAN-AFRICAN RIFT AND OTHER POEMS

Avoth Yeshurun

THE SYRIAN AFRICAN RIFT

AND OTHER POEMS ☙

Translated and with a foreword by HAROLD SCHIMMEL

The Jewish Publication Society of America · Philadelphia 5740/1980

Copyright ©1980 by The Jewish Publication Society of America
Translation Copyright © by The Institute for the Translation of Hebrew Literature Ltd., Tel Aviv
Hebrew text ©1974 by Sifrei Siman Kriyah, Jerusalem, and reproduced here by the courtesy of the author and the publisher
All rights reserved   First edition
Manufactured in the United States of America

Designed by Adrianne Onderdonk Dudden

Library of Congress Cataloging in Publication Data
Yeshurun, Avot.
    The Syrian-African rift, and other poems.
(Jewish poetry series)   English and Hebrew.
    Selections of ha-Shever ha-suri afrikani, with English translation.
    I. Schimmel, Harold. II. Title. III. Series.
PJ5054.Y48S54213   892.4'15   80-13630
ISBN 0-8276-0181-6
ISBN 0-8276-0182-4 (pbk.)

Acknowledgments

Dennis Silk and Varda Schimmel first listened to these poems in English. The former, convalescing in Motsa, read the entire manuscript and provided stimulus and suggestions. The latter's "perfect pitch" in matters of poetry was, once more, a guide. David Weinfeld shared with me the anecdotes that appear in the "Coda" of my Foreword, and a bottle of vodka on a warm spring night with Avoth Yeshurun.

My first Avoth Yeshurun translations appeared in 1969 in the bilingual journal *Oroth*, edited by Ada Zemach. She and the late "Aleph Daled" Shapir encouraged my readings in Hebrew letters.

Special thanks to The Institute for the Translation of Hebrew Literature, which supported my work and gave me a free hand in the making of this book.

H. S.

To the poet of another city, Edwin Denby
H. S.

Contents

Translator's Foreword   xi

POEM IN THREE   3
    The collection   3
    The watch   5
    The lover   7

ROCKET AND BIRD PLANT   9
    Rocket   9
    Bird plant   11

POEMS AT HOME   15
    The wild dove   15
    Spring   17
    Victim nest   17

A NOVEL WITHOUT CLOTHES   21
    "I wanted to reach a small case"   21
    Friday, 24 Tammuz 5733, 27 July 1973   25

THE SYRIAN-AFRICAN RIFT
    The poem on the eve of this day   29
    The poem on the Jews   29
    The poem on this day   31
    The poem on the guilt   33
    The poem on the Africs   33
    The poem on our Mother Our Mother Rachel   35

Quadruple   37

I walked like a horse   39

We hear his river   41

PLEASE DON'T ASK   43
    "A woman who was deserted"   43
    "My son my son I exiled"   45
    "I say hello"   47

PACKAGES   49
    Poem from Tel Aviv   49
    Lullaby for Nordia Quarter   53

THREE LITTLE-GIRL POEMS   57
    Poem no. one ("In anemone-plucking time in Sharona")   57
    Poem no. two ("The Gordon School in Sharona for horseback riding")   57
    Poem no. three ("No one around")   59

SEVEN ON THE RAIN   61
    One ("The rains saved")   61
    Two ("The plant was brought in")   61
    Three ("The opening rain")   63
    Four ("Lord of heaven")   63
    Five ("You, rain, alter")   67
    Six ("I don't meet my kind")   69
    Seven ("A stone tossed into the mire")   71

January 1st, night   73

Miniatures from Tel Aviv   75

LOCAL POEMS   77
    Growth   77
    End of summer   77
    Lull   83
    Tree   85
    Who comes from the stars   85

THE ROOF IS PALE FROM THE WORLD   89
    "The houses at home live in apartments"   89
    "I heard they beat the house"   89
    "Gravel sand and cement are building materials"   91
    "The roof they now close"   93
    "You can climb on every star"   95

Acriman   97

Who comes   103

Still early   105

TUNE STATE   107
    "I'm one horse"   107
    "Why are the lights in an uproar that were reflected from the
        water"   109
    "In forty-eight I sat in the strong point"   109
    "The water subsided in the river"   111

UNTIL 15 MAY 1974   113
    "It's exactly like a lizard that penetrated in autumn"   113
    "Ana ayisha"   115
    "For the camels of Ayun Kara"   115
    "I heard child Avyam"   117
    "On a dirt road"   117
    "The road that's between two parts of Dizengoff"   119
    "That day and I stand on Haifa shore and eat"   121

Notes   125
Chronology   131

Translator's Foreword

Poetry's advantage is always in the place and the time. The local and the immediate are cement bags on the head, air under the instep. They give a poet a sense of physical weight. His body takes up real space in a factual and limited place.

Pose is an amplification and a sophistication, pose is inherent in every separate retinal image. It implies arrangement by exclusion and disposition by inclusion.

The poet's presence swells by the exclusiveness of local geography. Hart Crane at the center of Brooklyn Bridge occupies it uniquely and forever. The convergence becomes historical, as of Catullus at Sirmio, William Carlos Williams at Paterson Falls, or Merce Cunningham and Company in the Grand Piazza at Venice.

So the footprints of the nineteenth-century English poets cling to the soil of Italy with an obstinacy and palpability as of dinosaur footprints. So Cavafy, "many years died," as Avoth Yeshurun might say, continues to haunt the streets and back alleys of Alexandria.

Language too is of this time and of this place. The neo-archaisms and localisms, the slang historical and contemporary, the newspaper lingo, the fashionable lisp or semi-stutter of, say, John Ashbery writing in Manhattan accurately date themselves.

"Volveran" of Lowell's *Notebook* transforms and overtakes its antecedent in Bécquer. Or, to put it differently, Lowell consciously inhabits the local Spanish grammar of Bécquer's magical word the way Merce Cunningham teases the gravitational pull under the singular stones of Piazza Grande.

2

The poet will neither relinquish what his hands once grasped nor cease to hold on to what his hands now grasp. He speaks in the language of his youth, the language of his father, and the language of his manhood, himself at his father's age then. He also appropriates the language of his children, for he must speak to them.

This tenterhook hold on words (for every poet is his own historical dictionary) often results in a non-"spoken language." The lingua franca of the poet is the product of a multiple vision or, as Avoth Yeshurun writes, paradoxically:

He spoke in a literary poetry.
He spoke in a spoken poetry...

The language of John Berryman's poetry is variegated, but the language is the man in all of its guises.

A justification for the poet speaking in more ways than one, or in many ways at once, is no more necessary than a justification of Picasso's multifarious image in the various self-portraits. Picasso is Picasso in the clothes of Velásquez or in the left-behind hat of Dora Maar.

Hugh MacDiarmid's "synthetic" dialect is perhaps a parable for the dialects of the poets of all languages.

3

Avoth Yeshurun, in the wide majority among Hebrew poets, assumed a language. A mother tongue, technically, was Yiddish. Yiddish, among the Jews of Eastern Europe, was always and quite literally *mamaloshn*, the language in which one first learned to speak: "Mamma."

Geographically, politically perhaps, Yeshurun also owed allegiance to the Polish of the state schools, the Polish idiom and abuse from the tavern door, the Polish of the printed text and the newapaper. Child of a people of small tradesmen, his lexigraphic world also swallowed up bits of other languages: Russian, the Hungarian of the wine dealers, German words from the books of the Hebrew Enlightenment—the Haskalah movement in Hebrew literature, which consciously and ambitiously sought the knowledge of the nations: the secular Other.

The pungent thingness of objects in Avoth Yeshurun's poetry keeps its loyalty to Yiddish. Hebrew seems not nearly so weighted in the naming of objects. A clearer, sharper, harsher light lent *things* in the world of biblical literature their proper perspective. They were disposed in a real and native landscape, they held shadow potential, and their colors blurred into the soft full spectrum of gray as the light from above of the great luminary descended. There, objects were tools or incidents in the lives and hands of the heroes.

Yiddish tends to animate its objects, they are fewer and seem more basic; they belong, like the hump to the hunchback. Weighted for life, they can speak out, imply, implore, command, direct. The linguistic anatomy of *things*, metaphorical in most languages, in Yiddish is factual. The eye of the needle or buttonhole, the leg of a chair and the face of a table or watch, laces, a buckle, nails and nail parings, a door, a window, a roof, the clod from a turned field or the stone, the cloud between you and the moon; what is near becomes relevant in its intimacy. Things in the *shtetl*-world of Yiddish tend to couple: bed and back, backside and bench, money and pocket, hammer and hand. Their hold is a life hold. For better or worse, one defends what one is close to. "He who loves his watch," Yeshurun's lover-poet writes, "loves to see the hour how much."

Avoth Yeshurun is loyal also to the intonation and gesturing of his mother tongue. Yiddish is anarchistic. A non-inflected language, it assumes the privileges of Latin and classical Greek. Word order is by disposition and by impulse. Words themselves are handled like familiar objects, disposed in the sentence like raisins in a sweet *kugl* or carp, or like rough-ground black pepper in a fiery *kugl* or carp.

Yeshurun carries over the feel of Yiddish into his Hebrew. He doesn't ask, he takes the new language in his hands. The mouth is pried open, as the mouth of a child at the hands of a doctor who knows what's good for the child more than the child can. When Avoth Yeshurun writes, "Fifteen there are million Jews graphomaniacs./Writer there is one," the syntax is decisive. Grammatical alternatives are held down, brutally, as a boy drowns a cat, and purposefully.

4

Arabic is incorporated as well, taken over whole. The word or phrase becomes an object. The Bedouin woman coming over the hill cannot speak Hebrew, neither biblical Hebrew nor Avoth Yeshurun's familiarized, battered, homely Yiddish-Hebrew. She speaks Bedoui-speak—just as the camel speaks camel and cannot be made into a giant humpbacked Polish sheep dog of attenuated neck.

Avoth Yeshurun's first book of poems, *On the Wisdom of Roads*, published in Tel Aviv in 1942 under his first name, Yechiel Perlmutter, was a tribute to the desert people. Almost anthropological in its focus, the poet leaves behind his "I" and enters desert paths on desert terms, with Hebrew as his medium, perhaps for the first time in modern Hebrew poetry. The musicality is camel walk, and goat bell, a jingle of beaten silver at the fringe of a robe, a slurp of well water and yowl at night of the jackal. The language is of the Bible, often with allusions to that pre-dispersion nomadic state of the ur-fathers, but freshly shorn, sent out naked like a lamb to Azazel.

Perlmutter's heroes and heroines are Eldin of the scorpion mustache, Chalima of the sharp retort, Mohánenah waiting for his mother, Nahima with her lover on the limping three-legged couch, and the patient native camels, "always stretch-necked." The Arab was part of the scene, and the young Perlmutter rubbed shoulder and smells, felt the attraction to that strangest of worlds, and the inherited weight of his essential disparity. If he was to love the Land entire, he was to love as well the Arab woman, and made her his song.

5

The adopted name came at about the time of the founding of the State of Israel. It was really the third change, for the diminutive Chi'el of his childhood took on the Sephardic accent when he touched land at Haifa and was reborn Yechi-el. Now the change was to be self-wrought, adopted, willed. The name — in literal translation, "the fathers are looking (at us)" — would be his blazon.

The initial shock of these young settlers from Poland and Russia at the white dunes, the enamel blue of the summer sky, the olive trees, pomegranates, wild grapes, palms, almonds, figs, and carobs, to Mediterranean noon behind peeling, painted slat shutters, Little Tel Aviv and the early communes, road work or competition with the Arab laborer in the orange groves, can best be felt in those now-classic watercolors of the 1920s. Artists like Yoseph Zaritsky, trained in Russian formalist academies, experienced second sight — the visible world had to be put down with clear eyes, quickly, like a letter home. Transparent color and pencil on yellowed and faded inferior paper and cardboard become the appropriate and authentic classicism of the *Yishuv*, the pre-state Jewish settlement. These remain the little temples hurriedly put up before the first enthusiasm was gone, like those grander structures at Paestum and Agrigento. But whereas the Greek colonists, still in the slap and flash of a familiar Mediterranean, worshiped the old gods, these young settlers had to take part at the birth throes of a god much of their own making.

There was guilt over parting scenes. Mother and Father became the base of a trinity whose apex was to be the Land, that is, the new return to the old homeland—Eretz Yisrael—still amazingly fresh, to be seen with a daring virginal glance. The break was so complete, only the imagination could deal with it. The old history could be rehearsed only up to the breaking point, rehearsed and re-rehearsed—the table set, the concerned and the stern faces, pleas, stubborness, will, counter-will, rebellion and parting.

The son was now the *chalutz*—pioneer—at a distance defensible only through a firm belief in Scripture. The traditional longing for Zion was now the Mother's longing for the absent son. The Zion of embroidered wall pieces was concretized with flesh of my flesh, blood of my blood. The pioneer held up his role with basic and prescribed pioneer stints. His skin took on new color. Khaki shorts, wide and full-pocketed, fell to the knees. The Land was swarming with activity, arrivals and some departures, brother meeting brother-come-of-age, with palpable evidences from what was home.

As personal history merged with state history, with geography, with topography, with botany, a change of address became synonymous with national growth. The voice of Little Tel Aviv breaks and deepens, with the poet's, into a middle-years' basso.

Municipal history can be read in the gradual transformation of Avoth Yeshurun's quatrain. Perlmutter's rimed, fresh-limed, symmetrical house (the word for house and stanza is identical in Hebrew) little by little crumples with the salt's bite, with the humidity, with the constant baking under a methodical sun, with eventual exhaust fumes from city buses, and Levantine indulgence.

The quatrain spills, opens, takes in prose, dialogue, grows asymmetrical—top-heavy, or sagging. It is undermined, extended, the roof is built on, television antennae poke out unselfconsciously. As do the city's signs and billboards, newspapers and libraries and theaters, speak in all languages (the waiter speaks seven, the laundress speaks five), so does Yeshurun's quatrain.

Cadenza

By instinct the milkman's horse eats the apple from the tree with three four leaves and a bit of the soft of the branch. The horse digests.

Like a horse in Tel Aviv desert—eats nails and spits rust. "Violence!" yells the poet, with frothing fury. To sing "The Song of the Sea" in an unpoetical language!

> Worth it to see how the moon
> enters a struggle with clouds.
> Stones and muscle in his hand till the fight is done
> and he comes out clean.
>
> And he sails from reality to reality.
> ("Friday, 24 Tammuz 5733, 27 July 1973")

The poet as horse, the poet as pig ("... the richest. / Eats everything. / Even glass"). The poet as moon struggling with clouds, the poet as beaten-dog.

Everything that is in the world is a parable of the poet. And the thread that binds from horse to pig to dog is the life within them. The opposite of alive is... to look up at blue skies, and see nothing. No assurance, no response, nothing at all—and so we die.

> A house is alive if all are well.
> A dog runs from some anger.
> From some whipping, from some insult, comes
> to the wall, smells life on the wall, and lives.
> ("I heard they beat the house")

All the world is a house. Eretz Yisrael is a house. What was left "back there" also a house. A man's house is a house and a man's house (the sages say) is his wife. "The margosa tree is the night house of the shadow. Because the shadow/ is a house."

> I took off the house.
> How did I wear the house?
> I left my mother.
> How did I take a wife?
> ("The road that's between two parts of Dizengoff")

"A bulldozer came kicked the house" is a parable of the destruction of the world. A parable of the poet who took leave of his father and mother. A parable of a woman who "Tosses on high the shorts"—

> Soon the nest will come down
> for processing....

> They won't build house?
> What will the wild doves do?
> Where will they lead the environment?
> Of course they'll build house.
>
> ("End of summer")

"What's important I lived," writes Avoth Yeshurun. "Between house and house earth."

> Punished Earth.
> You needn't start up with her. To speak
> to her you need. To trick out her wardrobe. As meadows
> wore sheep so we wore her the Land.
>
> ("The poem on our Mother Our Mother Rachel")

The poetics of Avoth Yeshurun imply an economical viewing of the world. The secret of his method lies in a dog smelling, a woman tossing, a moon sailing from reality to reality. Like his father who worked in flour mills:

> Surely he knew what is bread.
> His crumbs were on the table.
> Not under the table.
>
> ("Victim nest")

The poet in Avoth Yeshurun is a *weltmensch* (a house-owner in my translation). The poet as poor, wandering Jew, ragman, collector of assorted junk (*alte sachen*), scribbling accounts (like the God of the Jews):

> Wrote down and sealed and counted and numbered her.
> Like that.

"His crumbs" are all the words that give off smell. Groups of words! Poetry in small words ("And at the same time—/thwaak") and poetry in big words ("A comet will radiate its volcanic/ scar in the flame of a cooking stove").

Important, also, is the pose,

> the hands in the pockets of the pants.
> under the slash in the jacket.
> Observe: a stance of men.
>
> ("Acriman")

a pose that comes closer to the figure of Walt Whitman in his own eyes than to the dawdling urban dandy of Baudelaire. Another thing that puts Avoth Yeshurun close to Whitman is the always-right-tone—the most individual tone in Hebrew poetry. "There *are* no lost landscapes. There aren't. Already according to the technique of *fata morgana* there aren't."

The accent, the gesture in the voice, is his signature. His signature is also felt in his grammar ("In the warmth of the standing and the steam I dreamt: how much there was rain"), and in the rhythm of his walk through the poem:

> I walked in you everything by foot,
> like the horse eats straight from the earth.
> There are times I suffer martyrdom
> for every faucet you forgot open.
>
> ("Lullaby for Nordia Quarter")

The ambling poet (the poet as pedestrian) is also distinguished from the *flâneur* of Baudelaire by his optimism and by his full involvement and commitment. With all his kicking up of the heels Avoth Yeshurun remains a decided romantic. A plant, a bird, an abandoned woman, these are his typical and central themes:

> Wings pass from branch to branch
> a secret of transmission.
>
> ("The road that's between two parts of Dizengoff")

> If I tell you something day to night,
> it's love.
> If I tell you something night to night,
> it's love.
>
> ("Acriman")

And so, despite all the poet's virile proclamations as to the advantages of power (the poet as tough-guy!),

> In poetry you must use force.
>
> ("Poem from Tel Aviv")

> In poetry you must go with force.
>
> ("Poem from Tel Aviv")

> I opened the earth like a cow's muzzle.
> Like a horse lifting his muzzle from the fodder.
>
> ("I'm one horse")

there are among his quatrains the most slender, the most weightless, the most elegant things. See for example the delicate touch in the closure of the poem, "January 1st, night":

> Playing chess. The house
> café cram-full December.
> Listening to Joan Baez
> sing "I remember."

Coda

Coming out of a late show of a Japanese film, Avoth Yeshurun was stopped by a friend who extolled the Russian film he had just seen, *The Lady with the Toy Dog*.

"A shame," he said, "you had to miss Chekhov for Kurasawa!"

"The only difference between Kurasawa and Chekhov," Yeshurun countered, "is one eats rice, the other himself!"

And I would read the anecdote not as a matter of preference, but of the futility of this kind of choice. Somewhere in Yiddish there is surely a proverb pointing to the end of all eating; about intellectual pickings, Solomon made the point in that long chaotic harangue, *Koheleth*.

What matters is the manner of holding on to one's own. Thus, the style of the worshiper and not the inherent merits of the hero. The spiel has its ethic in emphasizing the way things are met and minimizing outcome. In Avoth Yeshurun's "A Novel Without Clothes" the whole weight falls on the delicious frenzy of the pursuit. We know little about the actual buckle or bookcase.

One insists upon one's own, like children slicing out pieces of earth according to the fall of the penknife blade in a game of "Territory."

Seeing a redhead friend pick something up from across the street, Avoth Yeshurun called out, "Hey, Redhead!" And crossing hurriedly, "Well, what did you pick up? Hand over!"

"It was a five-pound note," the redhead said. "Why?"

"This is my neighborhood," Yeshurun gestured, firmly, with his gray mane. "It belongs to me."

Needless to say, he won out and was five pounds richer. Moreover, he defended what was rightfully his: the neighborhood!

But can one defend his Hebrew through English? Ten years ago it would have been wild even to consider the notion of translation. But what has happened in English poetry these last years has made the way somewhat easier.

Beyond that, the reader of translated poetry today approaches it much the way the translator himself approaches his work. One reads to find what is new, what is advanced in poetic thinking—much the way Robert Lowell approached his first Montale versions about 1959 in Boston, or the way Michel Deguy went further back, to Gongora, during his sojourn in Spain about the same time.

For poetic technique is poetic wisdom, and Avoth Yeshurun would be delighted at the idea of young New Yorkers, Californians, or graduate-student poets in walled Chester reading him to get smart.

"Tel Aviv the holy city," he writes, placing it on the poetic map.

Translators usually aim their arrow at something like "faithfulness" without going so far as to appear "slavish"—a little like a Latin husband. I have taken over Yeshurun's own words (humbling) as my motto: "parrot paraphrase by precept." That is, admiring the poetry, I have felt inclined to take it whole. I have never glossed the odd or excised the difficult. I have tried to keep the difficulty (a closeness of thinking, or poetic argument, I have discovered) in.

The reader is urged to begin with the table of contents—the selections in the present volume are all taken from Avoth Yeshurun's *The Syrian-African Rift* (1974)—and read the poems in their series, as they were conceived. I'd launch the collection with some quatrains from "Bird plant":

> A dingdong plant sniffs out water for winter.
> A childhood plant the clock on the wall.
> Twelve musics ring from him.
> Goes on and arrives on time for the ding.
>
> A toy plant a childhood plant
> to inspire faith in the toy.
> Let the horse be of wood let the horse be flesh and blood.
> Important the boy without really trying lead them.

A rain ditch bird from the land of Naftali.
Isn't embarrassed by her surroundings.
Opens her wings accordion-like.
On one foot you spy her linen.

They're all looking
and she's looking.
They want to catch
and she's not caught....

Harold Schimmel
Jerusalem, 5739/1979

THE SYRIAN-AFRICAN RIFT
AND OTHER POEMS

שיר בשלושה

הָאֹסֶף

אֲנִי מֵבִיא כָּל מַה שֶׁאֲנִי מוֹצֵא.
לֹא כָּל מַה שֶׁנּוֹצֵץ הוּא זָהָב.
אֲבָל אֲנִי מֵרִים
כָּל
מַה שֶׁנּוֹצֵץ.

בִּמְגֵרָה אֹסֶף שֶׁל בְּלָאי.
חֲתִיכוֹת שֶׁל כְּרוֹם. מַפְתֵּחַ בְּלִי רַגְלַיִם.
מַסְמֵר מַרְבֵּה שָׁנִים. שֶׁאֲנִי רָץ מִן הַחוּץ,
כִּמְעָרָה חַיָּה מִסְתּוֹרִית, שֶׁאֲנִי חוֹצֶה בְּכֹחַ בַּמֵּצַח.

שֶׁאֲנִי כְּלִי בַחוּץ מַבִּיט. בַּכֹּל מַרְבֶּה עֵינַיִם.
חֲתִיכוֹת נִיקֶל, כְּרוֹם, בַּרְזֶל,
אֲנִי לֹא יוֹדֵעַ מִמַּה זֶה בָּא.
שִׁירֵי עֲצָמוֹת. שַׂעֲרוֹת רַגְלַיִם. מִמִּי הֵם?

כָּל זֶה מֻנָּח כַּאֲשֶׁר אֲנִי חוֹצֶה חוּצוֹת.
פִּתְאֹם בְּשָׂרֵנוּ מֵתְאוֹ מְכוֹנִיּוֹת, הַרְהוּרִים בַּדֶּרֶךְ, סְבוּב, מַלְכּוֹד, בַּרְזֶל נוֹפֵל מִן הַבּוֹ
כָּל אֶחָד אוֹמֵר שֶׁלּוֹ. כָּל אֶחָד מַבִּיט לִי בְּיָדַי.
לֹא כָּל מַה שֶׁנּוֹצֵץ הוּא זָהָב.

אֲבָל כָּל אֶחָד רוֹצֶה לֶאֱסֹף.
כָּל הַמַּפּוּל הַזֶּה, כָּל הַיְבָלֶת הַזֹּאת, כָּל הָאַרְבֶּהֲרֹשׁ הַזֶּה, לְהִכָּנֵס
לֶאֱסֹף. וַאֲנִי מֵרִים
כָּל מַה שֶׁאֲנִי מוֹצֵא.

POEM IN THREE

The collection

I bring everything I find.
Not everything that glitters is gold.
But I pick up
everything that glitters.

In the drawer an old-clo'-man's collection.
Bits of chrome. A key without legs.
A multiple-toothed nail. Which I run from outside,
like a cave strange beast, which I cross like an arrow in the brow.

Which I entirely outside watch. In everything multiple-eyes.
Bits of nickel, chrome, iron,
I can't tell from what it comes.
Leftover bones. Leg hair. From whom?

All this laid out when I cross streets.
Lessen our flesh from car lust, thoughts on the way, a turn, a trap,
    iron falls from the powers.
Everyone says *his*. Everyone stares me in the hands.
Not everything that glitters is gold.

But everyone wants for the collection.
All this floodfall, all this yield, all this weevilrat, to enter
the collection. And I pick up
everything I find.

השעון

הַשָּׁעוֹן שֶׁהִגִּיעַנִי הֶחָדָשׁ.
מָה אוֹמְרִים עָלָיו בְּשָׁרֵיִ"ן.
נִבְדָּל מִקּוֹדְמָיו בְּמַהְפֵּכָה אֲפֹרָה.
שָׁעוֹן בַּעַל סְפָרוֹת מְרֻבַּע רוֹמִיּוֹת עָגֹל.

הַלּוּחַ קַל. וּלְהַבְדִּיל קַל.
יֵשׁ מְחוֹגִים לְשָׁעָה גְּדוֹלָה
וּלְשָׁעָה קְטַנָּה, מָחוֹג מָחוֹג.
שָׁעָה שְׁלֵמָה מְחַכִּים

עַד בּוֹא הַשָּׁעָה הַגְּדוֹלָה.
וּבֵינְתַיִם הוֹלְכוֹת לְאִבּוּד
הַשָּׁעוֹת הַקְּטַנּוֹת.
זֶה בָּרוּר.

מַה שֶּׁקָּשֶׁה לְהָבִין אֵצֶל דָּג,
שֶׁעוֹמֵד חָשׂוּף וְשָׁקוּף בְּמִגְרָשׁ בְּשָׁקוּף הַמַּיִם.
וְאִלּוּ פִּתְאֹם הַמְּחוֹגִים מְפַרְפְּרִים כִּכְנַף אַחַר
הַשָּׁעוֹת הַקְּטַנּוֹת. זֶה בָּרוּר.

הַלּוּחַ בְּזֶה מַשֶּׁהוּ. מִיּוֹצְאֵי
יַלְדוּת שֶׁל שְׁעוֹנֵי
יַד קוֹדְמִים, שֶׁמְּחוֹגֵיהֶם
נֶעֶצְרוּ וְנֶעֶצְמוּ כְּעֵינַיִם.

הַשָּׁעוֹן עָגֹל, הַלּוּחַ בְּזֶה
וּפְנִימָה חַם.
וְסָבִיב יָם עָגֹל
וְחוּצָה קַר וְחַם.

The watch

The watch that did reach me the new one.
What do they say about it in Schweiz.
It differs from its antecedents by a gray revolution.
A watch with square Roman numerals that is round.

The face is simple. And simple to make out.
There are hands for large hour
and small hour, one each.
A full hour you wait

till the large hour comes round.
And meanwhile the small hours
are wasted.
That's clear.

What's hard to grasp with a fish,
that stays bare and transparent in the water's transparent.
Whereas suddenly the hands flutter like a wing after
the small hours. That's clear.

The face is beige somewhat. Offspring of
a childhood of antecedent
wrist watches, whose hands
stopped and shut like eyes.

The watch is round, the face is beige
and inside warm.
And all about a round sea
and outside cold and warm.

האוהב

הַשָּׁעוֹן הַזֶּה אֲנִי מַחֲזִיק אוֹתוֹ עַל הַיָּד.
וְהוּא מַחֲזִיק אוֹתִי עַל הַיָּדַיִם.
מִי יוֹדֵעַ כַּמָּה זְמַן, וְהוּא
יוֹרִיד אוֹתִי מִן הַיָּדַיִם.

הַלּוּחַ אִם אֵינֶנּוּ בְּזֵשׁ,
הַלּוּחַ הוּא קוֹדֵר.
מַרְאֶה אֵיזֶה שָׁעָה יֵשׁ.
הוּא אֵינֶנּוּ מִתְחַמֵּק.

הַשָּׁעוֹן הַזֶּה אֲנִי נוֹשֵׂא אוֹתוֹ עַל הַיָּד.
וּמַן הַזְּמַן פּוֹרְשִׂים עָלַי שׁוּלֵי יָדָיו.
מִי יוֹדֵעַ כַּמָּה זְמַן, וְהוּא
יֶאֱסֹף מִמֶּנִּי אֶת שׁוּלָיו.

פַּעַם הָיָה לִי עֵסֶק עִם שָׁעוֹן.
שׁוּב סְפָרוֹת מְרֻבָּעוֹת. מַרְבָּד רוֹמִי רוּסִיּוֹת מִן הַיַּלְדוּת.
וּמָה חָשַׁבְתִּי? הֶחֱזַרְתִּי לַשָּׂטָן.
הַשָּׁעוֹן עַצְמוֹ אָמַר: נָכוֹן. גּוֹאֵל חָזָק. דּוֹפֵק בְּךָ.

טוֹב תַּעֲשֶׂה, תִּקְנֶה חָבֵר.
חָבֵר אֱמוּנָה וְתִקְוָה. שָׁעוֹן
אֱמוּנָה וְתִקְוָה. שִׁירָה אֱמוּנָה וְתִקְוָה.
אִם אֵין שִׁירִים, הַשָּׁעוֹן מְנַצְנֵץ כִּגְבִיעַ.

מָקוֹם שֶׁאַתָּה מוֹצֵא חָבֵר,
אַתָּה מוֹצֵא שִׁירָתוֹ.
מִי שֶׁאוֹהֵב אֶת שְׁעוֹנוֹ,
אוֹהֵב לִרְאוֹת שָׁעָה כַּמָּה יֵשׁ.

The lover

This watch I keep him on the wrist.
And he holds me on the hands.
Who knows how long, and he'll
remove me from the hands.

The face if it isn't beige,
the face is gloomy.
Shows what hour it has.
It doesn't evade.

This watch I wear him on the wrist.
And from the time spread over me the edges of his hands.
Who knows how long, and he'll
collect from me his edges.

Once I had dealings with a watch.
Again square numerals. Square Roman Russian from childhood.
And what did I think? I'd been turned back to the devil.
The watch himself said: Right. A strong redeemer. Ticks in you.

Do well, buy a friend.
Friend of trust and of hope. Watch
of trust and of hope. Poetry of trust and of hope.
If there are no poems, the watch glitters like a chalice.

Where you find a friend,
you find his poetry.
He who loves his watch,
loves to see the hour how much.

רקטה וצמח ציפור

רקטה

הָעָצִיץ הַגָּדוֹל עוֹמֵד בְּמַצָּבוֹ. אַף עַל פִּי שֶׁכְּלִי רֵיק הוּא, הוּא חֶרֶס לֹא נִשְׁבָּר. אֵינוֹ עוֹמֵד בְּאֵיבָה כְּלַפַּי, רַק מַבִּיט לָרְחוֹב. וְהֶעָצִיץ הַקָּטָן, צַמֶּרֶת צַבְּרִית, קַרְנֵי אַיָּל, עוֹמֵד בֵּין שֶׁמֶשׁ וָאָרֶץ. זֹאת אוֹמֶרֶת: בֵּין זְרִיחָה וְחֶרֶס אֲדַמְדַּם, וּמַטִּיל צֵל הַצֶּמַח שֶׁהָיָה לוֹ. שֶׁהָיָה לוֹ וְאֵין לוֹ.

מַמָּשׁ נִשְׁבָּר הַלֵּב לְאֵיזֶה חֹרֶף נָפַל. מִיָּד פְּרָצִים אַלֶכְּסוֹנִיִּים שָׁלְחוּ עָלָיו רָקֵטָה. חַשְׁמַלִּים הִקִּיפוּ אֶת הַצֶּמַח. שָׁלְחוּ אַחֲרָיו אוֹר יוֹם. הַכֹּל. נִרְאָה מַה עוֹד יָבוֹא. רֶגַע נִתְרוֹקֵן הַגֶּשֶׁם. נָר הַשֶּׁקֶט. הֶעָלִים הֶחֱוִירוּ. נוֹצְצוּ כֹּחַ. רוּחוֹת הַדְּחִיפוּהוּ לְפָנָיו. הִצְלִיף פָּנִים עַל פָּנִים. אָז עָמַד הַצֶּמַח עַל רַגְלָיו קַדְמוֹנִית, בְּשׁוּר לוֹחֵם שְׁוַרִים, אֲשֶׁר שְׁפוּדִים כְּבָר בְּגַבּוֹ, כְּמַחֲטֵי קִפּוֹד, מַגִּנֵּי טֶבַע.

רָאָה בִּדְדִידוּתוֹ, רָאשֵׁי הֶעָלִים הוּעֲפוּ. רָאָה קָנֶה הַדַּק שֶׁלּוֹ, אָזְנָיו זְקוּפוֹת אֶל קָהָל פֶּרֶא. הִבִּיט עַל קָנֶה דַּק שֶׁלּוֹ, עַל חֹפֶן עָפָר שֶׁלּוֹ. בֵּין בִּצְבֵּץ בֵּין אֶצְבָּעוֹת וָבֹהֶן.

רָאָה אֶת לֹעַ הֶעָצִיץ. רָאָה אֶת הַלֹּעַ מִבַּחוּץ לֶעָצִיץ.

ROCKET AND BIRD PLANT

Rocket

The large flowerpot holds its own. Even though it's an empty vessel, it is clay unbreaking.
Does not hold me in enmity, just looks out at the street. And the small flowerpot, summit cactus,
ram's horns, holds out between sun and earth. That is: between sunrise and reddish
clay, and casts the shadow of the plant it had. That it had and hasn't.

The heart actually breaks for some winter fallen. Forthwith diagonal drafts sent on it a rocket.
Electricities surrounded the plant. Sent after it daylight. Everything. We'll see what's yet to come.
For a minute the rain emptied. Silence lives. The leaves paled. Sparkled power. Winds impelled it
forward. Lashed face upon face. Then the plant stood on its forelegs, like an ox
fighting bulls, with skewers already in its back, like hedgehog quills, nature's defense.

Saw its loneliness, the chief leaves were flown. Saw its thin stalk, its ears erect
to a wild crowd. Looked at its thin stalk, at its handful of dust. Mud bubbled between
fingers and thumb.

Saw the plant's throat. Saw the throat outside of the plant.

צמח ציפור

צֶמַח עָצִיץ דַּק קָנֶה נָפַל מִשָּׁם
אֶל הֶעָצִיץ הַגָּדוֹל עוֹמֵד רוֹקֵן
כְּמִבְצָר צַלְבָּנִי אֵיךְ לִהְיוֹת
עָצִיץ בְּלִי לְהִתְאַמֵּץ.

צֶמַח צַדִּיק. דֶּגֶל שִׂמְחַת תּוֹרָה. יוֹשֵׁב בַּטֶּבַע שֶׁלּוֹ.
שְׁלִישׁ אֲדָמָה. רְבִיעַ. עָפָר בִּנְבִיעַ.
אֵין לֶעָצִיץ הַגָּדוֹל אֲדָמָה לְהִתְחַפֵּר.
וְכֵן הַצֶּמַח אַדְמָתוֹ. וְאַדְמָתוֹ אַדְמָתוֹ. וְהַגְבִּיעַ אַדְמָתוֹ.

צֶמַח צִפּוֹר הוֹלֵךְ עִם סַעֲרוֹת הָעֵצִים.
אַל תִּסְתַּכֵּל עָלֶה נָגַף לְעֵינֶיךָ.
אֶחָד מֵהֶם נָפַל. עָלֶה נָגַף.
אַל תַּבִּיט מַה נָּגַף.

צֶמַח צִלְצוּל מֵרִיחַ מִמֶּנּוּ מַיִם לַחֹרֶף.
צֶמַח יַלְדוּת הַשָּׁעוֹן עַל הַקִּיר.
מְצַלְצֵל מִמֶּנּוּ שְׁתַּיִם עֶשְׂרֵה מוּזִיקוֹת.
וְהָלְאָה הוֹלֵךְ וּמַגִּיעַ בַּזְּמַן לְצִלְצוּל.

צֶמַח צַעֲצוּעַ צֶמַח יַלְדוּת
לְהָפִיחַ אֱמוּנָה בַּצַּעֲצוּעַ.
יְהֵא הַסּוּס מֵעֵץ יְהֵא הַסּוּס בָּשָׂר וָדָם.
חָשׁוּב הַיֶּלֶד בְּלִי לְהִתְאַמֵּץ נוֹהֵג בָּם.

צִפּוֹר שְׁלָחִין מֵאֶרֶץ נַפְתָּלִי.
אֵינָהּ מִתְבַּיֶּשֶׁת מִפְּנֵי הַסְּבִיבָה.
פּוֹתַחַת כְּנָפֶיהָ כְּאָקוֹרְדְּיוֹן.
עַל רֶגֶל אַחַת רוֹאִים לְבָנֶיהָ.

כֻּלָּם מִסְתַּכְּלִים
וְהִיא מִסְתַּכֶּלֶת.
רוֹצִים לִתְפֹּס
וְלֹא נִתְפֶּסֶת.

Bird plant

A thin-stalked flowerpot plant fell from there
to the big flowerpot emptying
like a Crusader fortress how to be
a flowerpot without really trying.

Pious plant. A Simchath Torah flag. Sits in its nature.
One-third earth. Quarter. Dust in the chalice.
The big flowerpot has no earth to dig itself in.
So the plant's its earth. And its earth its earth. And the chalice its earth.

A bird plant goes with the tree storms.
Don't look a leaf struck your eyes.
One of them fell. A leaf struck.
Don't look what struck.

A dingdong plant sniffs out water for winter.
A childhood plant the clock on the wall.
Twelve musics ring from him.
Goes on and arrives on time for the ding.

A toy plant a childhood plant
to inspire faith in the toy.
Let the horse be of wood let the horse be flesh and blood.
Important the boy without really trying lead them.

A rain ditch bird from the land of Naftali.
Isn't embarrassed by her surroundings.
Opens her wings accordion-like.
On one foot you spy her linen.

They're all looking
and she's looking.
They want to catch
and she's not caught.

כְּמוֹ בַּקַּיִץ שֶׁהָיָה עִם הָאֻזְדָּרֶכֶת.
נִכְנְסָה יוֹנַת בָּר לְבֵין עֲנָפֶיהָ.
הֵרִימָה זָנָב. הוֹרִידָה כְּנָפֶיהָ.
רָאוּ לְבָנָיהּ.

כֻּלָּם מִסְתַּכְּלִים
וְהִיא מִסְתַּכֶּלֶת.
רוֹצִים לִתְפֹּס
וְלֹא נִתְפֶּסֶת.

כָּךְ הַצֶּמַח בַּלַּיְלָה מַטְרִיָּה בַּשָּׁמַיִם.
בַּיּוֹם אַחַר הַלַּיְלָה מֻנָּח עַל הַמַּיִם.
בָּעֶרֶב מֻנָּח עַל הָעֶרֶב
וְנֶעְלָם מִן הָעַיִן.

Like summer past with the margosa tree.
A wild dove entered among its branches.
She lifted a tail. She lowered her wings.
They spied her linen.

They're all looking
and she's looking.
they want to catch
and she's not caught.

Thus the plant in night is an umbrella in the sky.
The morning after rests upon the water.
In the evening rests upon the evening
and is hidden.

שירים בבית

יונת הבר

בְּקַר הָעֵץ עוֹמֶדֶת יוֹנָה.
עוֹמֶדֶת עַל הָאַזְדָּרֶכֶת כִּפְרִי תָּפוּחַ
שֶׁנִּשְׁכַּח עַל הָעֵץ. וְהִנֵּה יוֹנָה
עוֹמֶדֶת עַל הָעֵץ.

כָּל פַּעַם שֶׁקַּר לָהּ הִיא מְסַבֶּבֶת
אֶת תַּחַת הַזָּנָב לַדָּרוֹם וְאֶת תַּחַת
הַמַּקּוֹר לַצָּפוֹן. רְעֵבָה – אֵין דָּבָר.
סוֹגֶרֶת עַיִן, פּוֹתַחַת – שׁוּב גֶּשֶׁם.

וַדַּאי הוֹנָה מַשֶּׁהוּ כְּמוֹ
בְּשֶׁלִּי בִּבְדִידוּת.
מַשְׁמִיעָה לֹא־בָּרוּר לֹא־נִשְׁמָע.
הִיא אוֹמֶרֶת זֹאת לְתוֹךְ הַזֶּפֶק.

קוֹלֶטֶת לְפִי הַנּוֹף פְּנִימָה
כָּל כַּמָּה שֶׁיְּכוֹלָה טִפּוֹת.
וּלְיֶתֶר –
לְיֶתֶר דִּיּוּק: נוֹזֶלֶת עַד קְצוֹת הַזָּנָב.

מִישֶׁהוּ הִדְלִיק בְּאַחַד הַחַלּוֹנוֹת הַחַשְׁמַל.
רְעָדָה קַל.
חָשְׁבָה בָּרָק.
הָלַךְ רַעַם.

לְיוֹנֵי בָּר אֵין דָּבָר אַחֲרֵי קָרְבַּן הַקֵּן.
רַק כְּשֶׁיֵּשׁ לָהֶם לֵדָה. כְּשֶׁיֵּשׁ
לָהֶם לֵדָה, זֶה יֵשׁ לָהֶם בַּיִת. אֵין
לֵדָה – אֵין בַּיִת. לָנִים בְּקוֹפִים עַל הָעֵץ הַקַּר.

הַגֶּשֶׁם תָּפַס אֶת הָעֲנָפִים,
שֶׁהֵם כְּבָר עֲגִילִים בַּבִּרְכַּיִם,

POEMS AT HOME

The wild dove

In the cold of the tree stands a dove.
Stands on the margosa tree like apple fruit
forgotten on the tree. And here a dove
stands on the tree.

Every time she's cold she turns
the bottom of the tail South and the bottom
of the bill North. She's hungry—no matter.
Shuts an eye, opens—rain again.

Surely she moans something like
in snow all alone.
Utters unclear unheard.
She says it into the crop.

Absorbs according to the body inward
just as much as she can drops.
And to be more—
to be more exact: leaks to the tips of the tail.

Someone turned on in one of the windows electricity.
She trembled a bit.
Thought lightning.
Tread thunder.

For wild doves there is nothing after the nest's destruction.
Only when they have a birth. When
they have a birth, why they have a house.
Birth—no house. They lodge like monkeys in the cold tree.

The rain gripped the branches,
which already are rounded like thighs,

וְשָׁרְשֵׁי הֶעָלִים חֲרִיצִים בְּלוּטִים.
בְּשָׁרְשֵׁי חָזֶה שֶׁל נַעֲרִיּוּת.

מָצָאתִי אֶת יוֹנַת הַבָּר מוּטֶלֶת עַל הַגַּב.
רַגְלֶיהָ אֲחוּזוֹת כְּתִינוֹק. כְּנָפֶיהָ גְּלוּלוֹת כִּגְלִילִים. הַגּוּפָה בָּאֶמְצַע.
יוֹנַת הַבָּר הִיא הֲכִי לֹא־קְרוּאָה.
וְאוּלַי זֹאת יוֹנָה אַחֶרֶת. קָשֶׁה לָדַעַת.

אביב

עֲטוּפֵי רֵיחַ וְלֵחוּת שֶׁל תִּינוֹקוֹת הָיוּ בָּאָבִיב.
כָּל מִינֵי הַחֲרָקִים הֵם אַךְ יָצְאוּ. הִתְרַשְּׁמוּ
מִן הַטְּרָפִים הַוְּרֻדִּים שֶׁעוֹד לֹא הִתְיַשְּׁרוּ
מִן הָרֶחֶם. וּמֵרֵיחַ הָרֶחֶם הַחֲרָקִים הִתְבַּשְּׂמוּ.

בָּעֶרֶב הָעֵץ מִתְעַבֶּה. הַחוֹרִים
נִסְתָּמִים עַל יְדֵי הָעֶרֶב. הַיָּרֹק נַעֲשֶׂה כֵּהֶה.
הָעֵץ מִתְחַזֵּק עִם הַלַּיְלָה לְאֶחָד.
הָעֵץ נַעֲשֶׂה עִם הָעֶרֶב מְעֻבֶּה יַעֲרוּת.

עַכְשָׁו הַטְּרָפִים מוּדָעֵי וַדָּאוּת שֶׁל גְּמַר בְּשׁוּלָם.
הָאַזְדַּרֶכֶת סוֹפֶרֶת אֶת הָעַלְעַלִּים עַל אֶצְבְּעוֹת הֶעָלִים.
זֶה הַמַּצָּב הַנָּתוּן עַד לְהַרְפַּתְקָה שֶׁל סְתָו.

קן קרבן

אָבִי הָיָה כָּל חַיָּיו עוֹבֵד בְּטַחֲנוֹת קֶמַח.
וַדַּאי יָדַע מַה־זֶּה לֶחֶם.
פֵּרוּרָיו הָיוּ עַל הַשֻּׁלְחָן.
לֹא תַּחַת הַשֻּׁלְחָן.

and the base of the leaves acorn grooves.
Like breast base of nymphets.

I found the wild dove placed on the back.
Her legs held like a baby. Her wings wound like spools. The trunk in
   the middle.
The wild dove is the most least-called.
And maybe this is another dove. Hard to know.

Spring

Wrapped in smell and damp of babies they were in spring.
All kinds of the insects they even emerged. They were impressed
by the pinkish blades that still hadn't straightened
from the womb. And from the smell of the womb the insects were
   perfumed.

In the evening the tree thickens. The holes
are plugged by the evening. The green becomes dark.
The tree is braced with the night to one.
The tree becomes with the evening thickened with foresthood.

Now the blades bear certainty of the end of their ripening.
The margosa tree counts the leaflets on the fingers of the leaves.
This is the given condition until autumn's adventure.

Victim nest

My father had all his life worked in flour mills.
Surely he knew what is bread.
His crumbs were on the table.
Not under the table.

הַשֻּׁלְחָן מִמֶּנּוּ אָכַלְנוּ כָּל הַשִּׁבְעָנָה
יָרַד מִמֶּנּוּ הַצֶּבַע חוּם וְעָלָיו
עוֹד הִתְגּוֹשְׁשׁוּ פֵּרוּרֵי
לֶחֶם שֶׁל אֲרוּחָה אַחֲרוֹנָה

בַּיּוֹם שֶׁעָזַבְתִּי אֶת הַבַּיִת אֲנִי
רִאשׁוֹן. הַשֻּׁלְחָן הָיָה מֻרְאָא וְהַפֵּרוּרִים
הָיוּ קְמוּטִים וַעֲצוּבִים כְּשַׂק הַיּוּטָה שֶׁמִּמֶּנּוּ לָקַח קֶמַח.
עַד שֶׁרָאִיתִי כֵּן תָּלוּי כְּקָרְבָּן עַל פְּתִיל אֶחָד

לָקְחוּ לָהֶם
בִּתְקוּפַת הֵרְיוֹנָם בַּחֲצֵרוֹת
וּמִסָּבִיב לַחֲצֵרוֹת מוֹךְ וּמַחַטִּים
וְהִתְיַשְּׁבוּ בַּמּוֹךְ

עַד שֶׁהוֹפַךְ מִן הֶעָנָף
בְּגֶשֶׁם פֶבְּרוּאָר שֶׁעָלָיו אָמוּר
לְמַלֵּא אֶת מֵאֲגַר הַכִּנֶּרֶת
הָיָה מֻנָּח עַד שֶׁנֶּעֱזַב

נֶחְשַׂף בַּשֶּׁמֶשׁ מֻנָּח
הָעוֹף וְעַד שֶׁהִגְלִישׁ
אוֹתוֹ סוּפַת הַגֶּשֶׁם פֶבְּרוּאָר וְתָלָה
אוֹתוֹ עַל פְּתִיל אֶחָד

בָּרוּחַ מִשְׁתּוֹבֶבֶת מוּל הַקֵּן הָרֵיק בְּכֹחַ עוֹדֵף.
בִּזְרִיקָה מוּל זְרִיקָה הוֹדֵף
אֶת מַה שֶׁהָיָה פַּעַם בֵּיתִי
כְּשֶׁאֲנִי הָיִיתִי בַּבַּיִת.

זֹאת אֲנִי מֵצִיץ מִצַּד חַלּוֹן אָבִי.
אַךְ לְמַעֲשֶׂה אֲנִי עוֹמֵד בַּחַלּוֹן שֶׁלִּי. וְיָבוֹא לָאָדָן צֹרֶךְ.
לְשַׁנּוֹת אֶת הַמַּנְעוּלִים. לְהַתְאִים אֶת הַדֶּלֶת
לַמַּשְׁקוֹף. עֲנָיִים הָיִינוּ בְּבֵית מִצְרַיִם.

The table from which we ate the whole sevensome
came off from it the brown color and on it
still wrestled bread
crumbs from a last meal

the day I left home I
first. The table was worried and the crumbs
were wrinkled and sad like the burlap sack from which flour was
    taken.
Until I saw a nest hung like a victim on one cord

they took themselves
in the time of their pregnancy in the yards
and about the yards down and needles
and settled in the down

until it was upturned from the branch
in February rain which is supposed
to fill the Kinnereth reservoir
it lay until abandoned

exposed in sun it lay
blown off and until the February
rain swamped it for good and hung
it on one cord

in wind raising Cain against the empty nest with surplus strength.
With throw against counter-throw
what was once my house
when I was home.

This I peer from the side of my father's window.
But in fact I stand at my window. And 'll come to the sill a need.
To alter the locks. To fit the door
to the lintel. Poor were we in Egypt home.

רומאן בלי בגדים

בִּקַּשְׁתִּי לְהַגִּיעַ לְאָרוֹן קָטָן.
בְּלִי סְפָרִים. שֶׁיִּהְיוּ הַמַּדָּפִים כֵּהִים
וְרֵיקִים. פֹּה וָשָׁם סֵפֶר. פָּשׁוּט
שֶׁיִּהְיֶה מְדַבֵּר אֵלַי.

אָרוֹן כָּזֶה הִגִּיעַ אֵלַי.
מוֹצָאוֹ מְשׁוּק הַפִּשְׁפְּשִׁים.
עוֹשֶׂה רֹשֶׁם כָּזֶה. מִכָּל מָקוֹם
קוֹדְמוֹ הַבַּעַל הָיָה בַּשּׁוּק.

הָיָה עַתּוּנַאי. לֹא מְשַׁנֶּה.
בְּעָזְבוֹ אֶת הָאָרֶץ נָתַן
מַתָּנָה. מִמַּתָּנָה לְמַתָּנָה, בְּמִדְבַּר מַתָּנָה,
הָאָרוֹן הַזֶּה הִגִּיעַ אֵלַי.

הוּא כַּנִּרְאֶה אָחַז סְפָרִים
דַּקִּים. סִפְרֵי שִׁירָה. אֵינוֹ מַקְפִּיד.
קַוִּים חַדִּים וּפְשׁוּטִים. סִדּוּר
תְּפִלָּה מְקוֹמִי. נָתַן לַהֲמָרָה.

כָּעֵת הוּא פָּנוּי מֵהֶם.
הוּא בִּפְנִיּוּתוֹ. מַה שֶּׁהָיָה
אֲנִי. הָיִיתִי מַשְׁאִיר אוֹתוֹ כָּךְ
לְעוֹלָמִים.

לְקַחְתִּיו בִּשְׁתֵּי אֶצְבָּעוֹת לְנַעַר
לְתַקֵּן רַגְלוֹ. וּלְפוֹלִיטוּרָה. לָמָּה לֹא? אָמְרוּ לִי:
שָׁמָּה. רְחוֹב שֵׁינְקִין. שָׁם. בֶּחָצֵר.
עָשָׂה עֲבוֹדָה טוֹבָה לְאִישׁ צַמֶּרֶת.

סַנְדְּלָרִיּוֹת, נַגָּרִיּוֹת, הַיּוֹם בְּיָמֵינוּ מִתְחַסְּלוֹת.
מִי יוֹדֵעַ אִם יַעֲשֶׂה. בִּבְרָק רִאשׁוֹן
אֲנִי עוֹד מַצְלִיחַ. אַךְ בְּמַבָּט שֵׁנִי,
מַפְסִיד. בָּאתִי וְאָמַרְתִּי: "תַּקֵּן אֶת

A NOVEL WITHOUT CLOTHES

I wanted to reach a small case.
Without books. The shelves should be dark
and empty. Here and there a book. Simply
it should speak to me.

Such a case reached me.
Its origin the flea market.
It looks it. Anyway
its predecessor the owner was in the market.

He was a journalist. Not that it matters.
When he left the country he presented
a gift. From gift to gift, in the desert a gift,
this case reached me.

It apparently holds books
thin ones. Poetry books. But doesn't insist.
Clear and simple lines. A local prayer
book. Convertible.

Now it's rid of them.
It in its riddance. What was once
me. I'd leave it that way
forever.

I took it with two fingers to a carpenter
to fix its leg. And for varnish. Why not? They told me:
there. Sheinkin Street. There. There. In the yard.
He did good work for a man of standing.

Shoemaker shops, carpentry shops, nowadays in our time are
    liquidating.
Who knows if he'll do it. In a first flash
I succeed even. But at second glance,
lose. I came and said: "Fix

הָאָרוֹן הַזֶּה וַעֲשֵׂה לוֹ פּוֹלִיטוּרָה.
שָׁמַעְתִּי לְאִישׁ צַמֶּרֶת אַתָּה עוֹשֶׂה
בְּעַד כֶּסֶף טוֹב." הַצִּלְצָל טָבַע
בְּרֹאשׁוֹ. הַנַּגָּר הִתְבַּלְבֵּל.

"תָּבוֹא בְּשָׁלוֹשׁ." עוֹד יֵשׁ לִי לִקְנוֹת
אַבְזָם לַחֲגוֹרָתִי. כְּבַחוּרָה
לַחֲבוּרָתִי. הַיּוֹם יוֹם הַשִּׁשִּׁי הַקָּצָר.
שָׁם בְּשִׁינְקִין. שָׁם שָׁם.

כַּפְתּוֹרִים מְתַקְתַּקִים. מַרְתְּקִים. הַזַּבָּנִית הַמּוּכֶּרֶת
הִבִּיטָה לִי בְּהֶחְלֵט לַחֲגוֹרָה וְנוֹתֶנֶת לִי אַבְזָם.
הִבִּיטָה בְּעֵין עֵינַיִם רַבּוֹא כַּפְתּוֹרֶיהָ. בָּחֲרָה אַבְזָם
וְאָמְרָה: זֶה אַבְזָם בְּעֵינֶיהָ.

חָזַרְתִּי לַנַּגָּר. וְעוֹד יוֹם. מִשָּׁם לִמְחַבֵּר אַבְזָמִים
לַחֲגוֹרוֹת. מִשָּׁם לְעוֹשֶׂה חֲרִירִים לַחֲגוֹרוֹת. עוֹשֶׂה
הַחֲרִירִים אִשְׁתּוֹ מֵתָה. נִשְׁאַר עֲרִירִי.
מִשָּׁם חֲזָרָה עִם הָאַבְזָם לַזַּבָּנִית וּמִשָּׁם לַנַּגָּר.

הָאָרוֹן עִם הַפּוֹלִיטוּרָה מוּכָן לַדֶּרֶךְ הָיָה.
לְקַחְתִּי אוֹתוֹ קַל בִּשְׁתֵּי אֶצְבָּעוֹת. "קַח אוֹתוֹ
אֵלֶיךָ לְמַעְלָה קַל בִּשְׁתֵּי אֶצְבְּעוֹתֶיךָ" הַנַּגָּר אָמַר.
וְכָךְ הָיָה הָאָרוֹן בְּלִי בְּגָדִים וְשִׁיר בְּלִי סְפָרִים.

נָסַעְתִּי לָאָרֶץ אָמְרוּ: זֶה נוֹסֵעַ לְפַלֶסְטִינִי שְׁמָמָה.
אֵיךְ זֶה הִתְקַשֵּׁר עִם פּוֹסְטִינְיָה שְׁמָמָה.
אֲנִי אוֹהֵב אֶת הַשְּׁמָמָה מִיּוֹם בָּאתִי
אֲנִי כְּאוֹהֵב אֶת הַיַּלְדָּה.

הִתְכַּנַּסְתִּי לָאָרוֹן וּבַחוּץ לַח בִּלְחָיַי אַנְיָה בִּשְׂפָם.
וּבִפְנִים אֲנִי וְגוּפִי אִינְטְשׁ אַחֲרֵי אִינְטְשׁ.
אֲרוֹנִי עוֹמֵד עַל שְׁנֵי שְׁבָבִים. הַגַּב דְּיֻקְט.
רַעֲמֵי שָׁמַיִם לַחֹרֶף מְזֻבָּנִים בְּפּוֹלִיטוּרָה וּבְדִיֻקְט.

וַאֲנִי בִּפְנִים מְכֹּחַ רֵיחַ הָעֵץ.
וַאֲנִי בִּפְנִים וְלִחְיַי בִּלְחִי הָעֵץ הַדּוֹמֶם לָאָדָם.

this case and varnish it.
I heard for a man of standing you'll do it
for good money." The ring drowned
in his head. The carpenter fumbled.

"Come at three." I still have to buy
a buckle for my belt. Like a gal
for my gang. Today is short Friday.
There on Sheinkin. There there.

Buttons tick. Gripping. The saleslady selling
looked me decidedly at the belt and gives me a buckle.
Looked with an eye of her myriad button eyes. Picked a buckle
and said: this is a buckle in her eyes.

I returned to the carpenter. It's still day. From there to the buckle fastener
for belts. From there to the hole-puncher for belts. The hole-
puncher's wife died. He remains forlorn.
From there back with the buckle to the saleslady and from there to the carpenter.

The case with varnish was ready to go.
I took it easy with two fingers. "Take it
up to your place easy with two fingers" said the carpenter.
And so the case was without clothes and poem without books.

I went to the Land they said: This one to Palestini wilderness.
How it connected with Pustinyeh wilderness.
I like the wilderness from the day I
came as I like the birth.

Snug in case and outside damp like the cheeks of a ship at the mustache.
And inside me and my body inch after inch.
My case stands on two chips. The back veneer.
Sky-thunder for winter blamms on the varnish and on the veneer.

And I'm inside by strength of the wood smell.
And I'm inside and my cheek's like the wood cheek, mum to man.

וְאַף עַל פִּי שֶׁאֲנִי גָּדוֹל מְמַדִּים
וְהָאָרוֹן קָטָן מְמַדִּים.

יֵשׁ לָאָרוֹן הַזֶּה יוֹתֵר מִשֶּׁאִישׁ
יָכוֹל לְשַׁעֵר אֶנֶרְגִּיָה.
אֵינִי חַיָּב לְאִישׁ מְאוּמָה לֹא.
אוּלַי פְּרָט אַחֲרוֹן הָרֶנֶע.

יום ששי, כד תמוז תשל"ג, 27 יולי 1973

אָבִי וְאִמִּי
אֶהֱיֶה מְשַׁמֵּשׁ אֶתְכֶם.
אֵין בֵּינֵיכֶם לְבֵין הַיֶּלֶד הַזֶּה
אֶלָּא אֲנִי לְבַד.

הוּא אַחַד הַיְלָדִים.
אָהֲבַת הֶחָצֵר אֶת הַמּוֹלָד.
נוֹגֵעַ בַּפַּפִּי שֶׁלּוֹ כְּתוֹלֵשׁ אֶת הַדֶּרֶךְ שֶׁלּוֹ
מֵהַלֶּחֶם שֶׁלּוֹ.

אָז אֲנִי לוֹקֵחַ לְהַרְאוֹת לוֹ
אֶת הַיָּרֵחַ כְּפִי שֶׁיֵּשׁ לִי
אוֹתוֹ בַּזִּכָּרוֹן מֵהַטִּיּוּל הָרִאשׁוֹן שֶׁלִּי
לְיָם הַמֶּלַח.

וְהָרֶשֶׁם שֶׁלִּי, כַּאֲשֶׁר אִישׁ
לֹא רוֹאֶה, הוּא יוֹרֵד מִלְמַעְלָה,
עוֹמֵד עַל בְּלִימָה, לֹא
מִשְׁתַּמֵּשׁ בְּשָׂפָה, אֶלָּא כִּמְדַבֵּר.

שָׁט יָרֵחַ שָׁם הֲכִי גָּדוֹל לָאֲדָמָה,
עַד אָז לֹא הִצְבִּיעוּ עַל הַפּוֹסְפָטִים,
וְלֹא הָיוּ סַמִּים וְלֹא הָיָה מָוֶת.
דָּבָר אֶחָד כֵּן: הָיָה לָנוּ פַּח מַיִם.

And despite the fact I'm big-sized
and the case is small-sized.

This case has more than man
can assume Energy.
I don't owe anyone anything no.
Perhaps last detail just now.

Friday, 24 Tammuz 5733, 27 July 1973

My father and my mother
I will serve you.
There is nothing between you and this boy
but me alone.

He's one of the natives.
The courtyard's love of the new moon.
Touches his weewee like plucking his soft
from his bread.

So I take to show him
the moon as I have
it in memory from my first hike
to the Dead Sea.

And my impression, when a man
doesn't see, he comes down from up,
stands on nothingness, doesn't
use language, except as a speaker.

Sails a moon there the biggest to earth,
till then they hadn't voted on the phosphates,
and there wasn't drugs and there wasn't death.
One thing yes: we had a water can.

תִּרְאֶה תִּרְאֶה מִן הָעֲרָבָה מִתְרוֹמֵם לְאַט,
עוֹבֵר אֶת מַחְסוֹם הָרֶכֶס,
עוֹבֵר תַּחַת עָשָׁן תַּחַת עָנָן,
עוֹבֵר מִמְּצִיאוּת לִמְצִיאוּת.

אֲנַחְנוּ הוֹלְכִים,
הוּא הוֹלֵךְ.
אֲנַחְנוּ עוֹמְדִים,
הוּא עוֹמֵד.

וְהָרִשּׁוּם שֶׁלִּי,
כַּדּוּר הַלֶּכֶת סָגוּר כַּחֲנוּת.
רַק הָאֲדָמָה מְרִימָה עֵינַיִם מִן הַמָּוֶת.
יָרֵחַ מוּכָן עוֹמֵד. מְחַכֶּה לָלֶכֶת.

לִפְנֵי שֶׁצְּרִיכִים לָלֶכֶת לִישֹׁן
וַאֲנִי צָרִיךְ
אֲנִי לוֹקֵחַ לְהַרְאוֹת לוֹ אֶת הַיָּרֵחַ.
וְעָנָן לוֹקֵחַ. חִבִּיתִי בְּקֹצֶר לְעָנָן שֶׁיֵּלֵךְ.

מִן הַמָּלֵא הוֹלֵךְ.
מִן הַחֲצִי.
מִן הַשְּׁלִישׁ.
מִן הָרְבִיעַ. וּכְבָר שֶׁיֵּלֵךְ.

כְּדַאי לִרְאוֹת אֵיךְ יָרֵחַ
נִכְנָס לְמַאֲבָק עִם עֲנָנִים.
אֲבָנִים וּשְׁרִירִים בְּיָדוֹ עַד שֶׁהַקְּרָב נִגְמָר
וְהוּא יוֹצֵא נָקִי.

וְהוּא שָׁט מִמְּצִיאוּת לִמְצִיאוּת.
עַל עֲיָרָה וְעַל שֶׁלֶט חֲנוּת
בּוֹ כָּתוּב בְּמִקְרֶה לוֹקֵשׁ בְּזִילְקוֹ. מִן הַיַּלְדוּת.
זֶה יוֹתֵר אֲנֶרְגְיָה מֵאֲשֶׁר פְּרָט אַחֲרוֹן הָרֶגַע.

Look look from the desert rises slowly,
passes the barrier of the ridge,
passes under smoke under cloud,
passes from reality to reality.

We go,
it goes.
We stand,
it stands.

And my impression,
a sphere that goes is closed like a shop.
Only the earth lifts eyes from death.
A ready moon stands. Waits to go.

Before we have to go to sleep
and I have to
I take to show him the moon.
And a cloud takes. I waited impa' for the cloud to go.

From full it goes.
From half.
From third.
From quarter. Just go already.

Worth it to see how the moon
enters a struggle with clouds.
Stones and muscle in his hand till the fight is done
and he comes out clean.

And he sails from reality to reality.
On town and on signboard
where is written by chance Lukacz Basilco. From childhood.
It's more energy than last detail just now.

השבר הסורי אפריקני

השיר על ליל היום הזה

חֲכָמִים אוֹמְרִים, כִּי בְּעֵת הִתְרַחֵשׁ הַשֶּׁבֶר הַסּוּרִי
אֲפְרִיקָנִי, שׁוֹכְנֵי הַמְּקוֹמוֹת לֹא הָיוּ
מֻעְדָּכְנִים. עָסַק אִישׁ
בִּמְלַאכְתּוֹ. בִּשְׁחִיזַת גַּרְזִנִּים. בִּבְקוֹעַ חַיּוֹת.

אֱנוֹשִׁיּוּת קְדוּמָה וְאֶרֶץ קַרְדֻּמָּה.
וּבִרְצוֹת אֵלֶּה אֵיזֶה שִׁנּוּי בָּאֲדָמָה
צְרִיכִים לַעֲשׂוֹת זֹאת בְּאֶמְצָעוּת הַרְדָּמָה.
לְאַחַר מִכֵּן מְעוֹרְרִים אֶת הָאֲדָמָה.

כְּמוֹ שֶׁעָשׂוּ לִי פַּעַם בִּבְדִידוּת בְּנַרְקוֹזָה
תַּחַת הַדְּרִיקְט וְהָנָג
בְּבֵית חוֹלִים בִּילִינְסוֹן: "יְשֻׁרוּן, עָבַרְתָּ נִתּוּחַ!"
הִנְנִי כָּאן. יוֹם הַכִּפּוּרִים.

השיר על היהודים

רֹאשׁ הַקָּהָל כָּאן עוֹמֵד בְּרֹאשׁ
שׁוּרָה אֲרֻכָּה שֶׁל קָהָל שֶׁעוֹמֵד מֵאַחֲרָיו.
שׁוּרָה יוֹתֵר אֲרֻכָּה מִזּוֹ שֶׁהָלְכָה וְאֵינֶנָּה.
שֶׁמִּי שֶׁלֹּא רָאָה אוֹתָהּ,

הוֹלֵךְ אֶצְלוֹ וְנִשְׁכַּח הַמַּרְאֶה וְאֵלּוּ
הַלָּלוּ אֲנָשִׁים, שֶׁאִם לֹא לְהִשְׁתַּמֵּשׁ בִּכְטוּיִים
אַל אֱנוֹשִׁיִּים, הֲרֵי אֶפְשָׁר לוֹמַר
בְּמִלָּה אַחַת: הֵם הָיוּ הַגְּדוֹלִים כְּשֶׁאָנוּ הָיִינוּ קְטַנִּים.

עַל יָדָם נֶחְתַּךְ כָּל דָּבָר אֲפִלּוּ חָתְכוּ
אֶת פְּרוּסוֹת הַלֶּחֶם שֶׁלָּנוּ וְחָתְכוּ לָנוּ

THE SYRIAN-AFRICAN RIFT

The poem on the eve of this day

The sages say, that at the time the Syrian-African Rift
occurred, the celestial inhabitants were not
up-to-date. Each man was engaged
at his trade. In grinding hatchets. In splitting beasts.

Ancient humanity and land of the axe.
And when those wanted some change on the earth
they have to do it by putting to sleep.
After that they waken the earth.

Like they did to me once in isolation in narcosis
under the plywood and the roof
in Beilinson Hospital: "Yeshurun, you underwent an operation!"
And here I am. Yom Kippur.

The poem on the Jews

The head of the congregation here stands at the head
of a long line of congregants who stand behind him.
A longer line than the one that departed and isn't.
Which—someone who has not seen it,

gradually the sight eludes him whereas
those other people, if not to resort to inhuman
idioms, why it can be said
with one word: they were the big ones when we were small.

At their hands each thing was cut they even cut
our slices of bread and they cut us

חֲצִי תַפּוּחַ שָׂאֵת קוֹל הַתַּפּוּחַ שָׁמַעְנוּ בִּשְׁעַת הַחֲתִיכָה.
וְנָגְעוּ בִּלְחָיֵינוּ וְקָרְאוּ שְׁמוֹתֵינוּ.

הֵם הָיוּ בְּמַעְגַּל סָגוּר הַיְּהוּדִים הַעִבְרִיִּים הַחֲבִיבִים עָלֵינוּ.
בְּחַגִּים וּבְשַׁבָּתוֹת. בְּכֹחַ עָרְכוּ
תְּפִלּוֹת וְזִמְּרוּ זְמִירוֹת וְהִכִּירוּ אֶת אֱלֹהִים.
וּבְבוֹא יוֹם כִּפּוּר הֶחֱזִיקוּ חֲבִילוֹת אֹכֶל בִּשְׁבִילֵנוּ בִּשְׁעַת הַצּוֹם.

אַחֲרֵי הַחַג הִתְגַּעְגַּעְנוּ עוֹד עַל אוֹתוֹ חַג וְעַל
אוֹתָם יְהוּדִים לִרְאוֹתָם יַחַד. טוֹב לִהְיוֹת בֵּינֵיהֶם שֶׁהֵם אֻמָּה
אַחַת שֶׁלֹּא מִשְׁתַּנִּים וְלֹא יָעִירוּ כֹּל חֲמָתָם וּמַבִּיטִים
עָלַי כְּמִי שֶׁלֹּא רָאוּ זְמַן.

השיר על היום הזה

הוּא עָמַד לִפְנֵי הַתְּפִלָּה וְלִפְנֵי הַזִּמְרָה.
אֲנִי עָמַדְתִּי לִפְנֵי הַסַּף. מִישֶׁהוּ מִתְפָּרֵץ:
יֵשׁ פֹּה מִקְלָט?
יֵשׁ פֹּה מִלְחָמָה.

פְּלוּצִים נִפְתְּחָה דֶּלֶת.
אֲנִי לִפְנֵי הַסַּף. יוֹם
זֶה, בּוֹ נוֹלַדְתִּי
לִפְנֵי תְּפִלַּת נְעִילָה,

יוֹם כִּפּוּר. זֶה בֵּינֵינוּ.
צַלָּמֵי־רוֹמֵיאוֹ־וְיוּלְיָה־קוֹלְנוֹעַ,
עַכְשָׁו כַּתָּבֵי חוּץ, יַצִּיגוּהוּ:
יוֹם כִּפּוּר אוֹ יוֹם הַדִּין.

רַבִּי שְׁמוּאֵל אֵלִיָּהוּ מִמּוֹדְזִיץ חוֹלֵק דִּמְעָתוֹ לִבְנֵי אָדָם.
הוּא עָמַד בִּתְפִלָּה וּבְזִמְרָה.
שַׂמְתִּי לֵב עַל כָּךְ. הִכֵּיתִי כַּף אֶל כַּף
וְיָצָאתִי בְּזִמְרָה.

half an apple which voice of the apple we heard at the cutting.
And touched our cheeks and called our names.

They were in a closed circuit the masculine Jews we adored.
On holidays and on Sabbaths. With force they conducted
prayers and chanted hymns and acknowledged God.
And when Yom Kippur came kept packages of food for us at the fast.

After the holiday we still longed for the same holiday and
the same Jews to see them together. It's good to be among those who
    are one
people who neither change "nor all their wrath awaken" and look
upon me as someone they didn't see awhile.

The poem on this day

He stood before the prayer and before the singing.
I stood before the threshold. Someone bursts out:
Is there a shelter here?
There's a war here.

Plump a door opens.
I'm before the threshold. This
day, on which I was born
before "Closing Prayer,"

Yom Kippur. It's between us.
Romeo-and-Juliet-photographers-cinema,
now foreign correspondents, will formally launch it:
Yom Kippur or Day of Judgment.

Rabbi Shmuel Eliahu of Modzitz apportions his tear to men.
He stood in prayer and singing.
I noticed that. I beat palm to palm
and came out singing.

השיר על האשמה

בָּרְכִי אִמִּי כִּרְכִּי יָדֵךְ עַל רֹאשִׁי בְּלֵיל
יוֹם זֶה. הָיִיתִי מֶה הָיִיתִי עוֹשֶׂה
לְיוֹם כָּפוּר. עֲיָרוֹת מִתְרַסְּקוֹת וְאַתְּ בִּפְנִים וְלַמֶּרְכָּז
הָאָרֶץ הַנְּשָׁמָה שֶׁלָּךְ וְהַגּוּף הִתְגַּעְגַּעְתְּ וְלֹא הִגַּעַתְּ.

אָבִיךְ בָּא בַּחֲלוֹם לָךְ.
פָּתַח אֶת אֲרוֹן הַזְּכוּכִית. שָׁבַר לָךְ כּוֹס. נִפְטַר לָךְ יֶלֶד
וְשָׁאַלְתְּ לָמָּה. אָבִיךְ לֹא עָנָה וְיָצָא וְחָשַׁבְתְּ לְכַפֵּר
וְשָׁכַבְתְּ עַל הָרִצְפָּה וְשִׁכַּבְתְּ עַל הַיֶּלֶד וְמָתָה מְנֻעְנֶעִים.

השיר על האפריקים

פְּלוּצִים נִפְתְּחָה דֶּלֶת. חַיָּל מָשַׁךְ אִישׁ מִלּוּאִים הַחוּצָה.
פָּשַׁט אֶת הַטַּלִּית מֵרָחוֹב לָרְחוֹב וּמְקַשֵּׁב לְסִפּוּר הַחַיָּל.
הָלַךְ עִם הַחַיָּל חָתוּל וְחָתוּל
וְלֶחִי וְלֶחִי.

הָלְכוּ שְׁנֵי הַמִּלּוּאִימְנִיקִים אֶל הַשֶּׁבֶר
הַסּוּרִי אַפְרִיקָנִי: בָּאתָ אֵלֵינוּ לִבְרֹחַ מִן הַלָּבָן.
אֲבָל שֶׁאַתָּה תִּהְיֶה הַנָּבָל? מָאוּס לִי הַמָּוֶת
כִּי אַפְרִיקִי בְּיָדֶיךָ.

יֵשׁ לָנוּ בְּעָיָה שֶׁל עֲקֵדַת יִצְחָק.
וְלָכֶם, כְּסָבוּר, עֲקֵדַת יִצְחָק.
לָנוּ זֶה יוֹצֵא כְּרַחֵם אָב עַל בָּנִים.
לָכֶם זֶה יוֹצֵא כְּרַחֵם אָב עַל עַצְמוֹ.

The poem on the guilt

Blest be Mother bind your hand on my head on the eve
of this day. I would have what would I have done
for Yom Kippur. Forests crash and you inside and at the center
of the land your soul and body you longed and did not arrive.

Your Father came in a dream to you.
Opened the glass cupboard; broke you a glass. A child of yours died
and you asked why. Your Father didn't reply and went out and you
    meant to forgive
and lay on the floor and lay on the child and died of longing.

The poem on the Africs

Plump a door opens. A soldier pulled a reservist outside.
Straightened the *tallith* from street to street and listening to the soldier's
    story.
Walked with the soldier cat and cat
and cheek and cheek.

The two reservist guys went to the Syrian-
African Rift: You came to us to escape the white.
But you be the villain? Loathsome to me is death
because an Afric's in your grip.

We have a problem of a sacrifice of Isaac.
And yours, you're inclined to think, the sacrifice of Isaac.
For us it comes out as a father has mercy on children.
For you it comes out as a father has mercy on himself.

השיר על אמנו רחל אמנו

וַיֵּלְכוּ שְׁנֵי הַמְּלוּאִים־מְנִיקִים. תִּרְאוּ, אַל תִּירְאוּ.
וַיִּשָּׂא יַעֲקֹב רַגְלָיו וַיֵּלֶךְ אַרְצָה בְּנֵי קֶדֶם.
וַיֹּאמֶר לָהֶם יַעֲקֹב: בֶּן־גּוּרְיוֹן וְנֶחֶמְיָה אַרְגּוֹב, אַחַי מֵאַיִן אַתֶּם?
לְבֶּן־גּוּרְיוֹן וְנֶחֶמְיָה אַרְגּוֹב אֵין תְּגוּבָה וְאֵין תְּשׁוּבָה וַיֵּלְכוּ שְׁנֵיהֶם.

צְרִיף שֶׁל בֶּן־צְבִי מְנוֹרַת עֵץ
מְקוֹמֵי פְּתוּחִים שֶׁל בָּתֵּי הַלִּישַׁנְסְקִי,
וְלֹא צִיּוּר עַל כָּל צִיּוּר וְלֹא שֶׁאַנְאַל
עַל כָּל צָרְפַת וּבֵית נָשִׂיא שִׂישׂוּ וְשִׂישׂוּ.

בִּפְנִים יוֹשֵׁב יַעֲקֹב.
עֵשָׂו עוֹמֵד בַּחוּץ.
בְּעַד הַחַלּוֹן נִשְׁקְפָה וַתִּתְיַצֵּב
אִם עֵשָׂו בְּעַד הָאֶשְׁנָב.

אֲדָמָה מְסֻנֶּפָה.
לֹא צָרִיךְ לְהַתְחִיל אַתָּה. לְדַבֵּר
בָּהּ צָרִיךְ. לְהַדֵּר בִּלְבוּשָׁהּ. כְּמוֹ כָּרִים
לָבְשׁוּ צֹאן כֵּן לָבַשְׁנוּ אוֹתָהּ אֶרֶץ.

אַל תִּקְרְאוּ לָהּ בְּשֵׁמוֹת רַבִּים.
קִרְאוּ לָהּ רָחֵל.
אָדָם נוֹלָד כְּיֶלֶד וָמֵת כְּיֶלֶד.
כָּל זֶה בְּסָמוּךְ לָאֵם.

אֲדָמָה מְסֻנֶּפֶת.
לֹא צָרִיךְ לְהַתְחִיל אַתָּה. לְדַבֵּר
בָּהּ צָרִיךְ. לְהַדֵּר. כְּמוֹ כָּרִים
כֵּן לָבַשְׁנוּ אֶת הָאָרֶץ הַזֹּאת.

The poem on our Mother Our Mother Rachel

And the two reservist guys went. Look, don't shoot.
And Jacob lifted his legs and went to the land of B'nei Kedem.
And Jacob said unto them: Ben-Gurion and Nechemiah Argov, my
    brothers from Whence?
From Ben-Gurion and Nechemiah Argov no reaction no response and
    the two went off.

Ben-Zvi's shack a wooden candelabrum
of local-make carvings by Batia Lishanski,
and not a painting on every painting and not Chagall
on every France and presidential mansion rejoice and rejoice.

Inside sits Jacob.
Esau stands outside.
From the window looks and wails
Esau's Mother from the lattice.

Punished Earth.
You needn't start up with her. To speak
to her you need. To trick out her wardrobe. As meadows
wore sheep so we wore her the Land.

Don't call her by many names.
Call her Rachel.
A man is born as a child and dies as a child.
All this dependent on the Mother.

Punished Earth.
You needn't start up with her. To speak
to her you need. To trick out. As meadows
so we wore this Land.

רְבַּעַת

נִמְלָא כִּיסִי בִּצְפִיפוּת
פִּתָּה צְפוּפָה. תְּפוּחָה
כִּגְלִימַת כְּפָר בַּחֹרֶף.
הֲפוּכָה בַּבֶּטֶן. תְּפוּרָה
כִּמְעִיל חַרְפִּי מְרֻפָּד.
הֲפוּכָה הַבֶּטֶן בַּחוּץ.
תְּפוּרָה רְבוּעַ וְרֻבַּעַת.

אָבִיתִי אֶת הַפִּתָּה
גַּם שֶׁל אָבִי.
הִסְתַּכֵּל אָבִי כִּי
כִּיסִי מָלֵא. וְהָלַךְ.
הָפַכְתִּי אֶת עֵינִי,
אָבִי עוֹד עוֹמֵד.
עַד כָּאן הַחֲלוֹם.

מִי יוֹדֵעַ בְּאֵיזֶה
וַאדְיוֹת אָבִי עוֹד.
מִזֶּה שֶׁלֹּא נָתַן
לִי אֶת הַפִּתָּה
אָבִי עוֹד עוֹמֵד.
בַּעַל חֲרָטָה אָנוּשׁ.
אוֹכֵל מִן הָאֶצְבָּעוֹת.

אֱמֶת, לֹא הַרְבֵּה
אֲנִי חוֹלֵם עָלָיו.
אֲנַחְנוּ עוֹמְדִים בַּתְּעָלָה.
וּמִי יוֹדֵעַ בְּאֵיזֶה
וַאדְיוֹת אָבִי עוֹמֵד.
הַרְבֵּה הָיִיתִי נוֹתֵן
לָדַעַת הַמָּקוֹם אֵיפֹהוּ.

דַּי שֶׁלֹּא נָתַן
לִי אֶת הַפִּתָּה,
עוֹד עוֹמֵד וּמִתְחָרֵט.
אָנוּ עוֹמְדִים בַּתְּעָלָה.
אֵיפֹה אָבִי עוֹמֵד?
הָיִיתִי הַרְבֵּה נוֹתֵן,
לְפֵשֶׁר בֵּין הָעֲמָדוֹת.

Quadruple

My pocket filled compact
with compact pita. Bulged
like a village robe in winter.
The lining inside out. Stitched
like a padded winter coat.
The lining inside out outside.
Stitched square and quadruple.

I desired the pita
also of my Father.
My Father observed that
my pocket was full. And left.
I turned my eyes,
my Father still stands.
Till here the dream.

Who knows in what
wadis my Father is still.
In that he didn't give
me the pita
my father still stands.
With mortal regret.
Eats from the fingers.

True, I don't often
dream about him.
We stand at the Canal.
And who knows in what
wadis my Father stands.
I'd give a lot
to know where stands he.

Enough he didn't give
me the pita,
he even stands and regrets.
We stand at the Canal.
Where does my Father stand?
A lot I'd give,
to mediate between the lines.

הלכתי כסוס

הָלַכְתִּי בַּגֶּשֶׁם,
כְּרְבוֹא סוּס.
עַל כַּפְתּוֹר אֶחָד
רִבּוֹא גֶּשֶׁם.

עַל הַסַּפְסָלִים בַּכְּבָר וּבַשְּׂדֵרָה הָלַךְ הַגֶּשֶׁם.
הִתְעַיַּפְתִּי.
הֶחֱלַפְתִּי רֶגֶל בְּרֶגֶל
וְנִרְדַּמְתִּי בַּעֲמִידָה.

עַד אֲשֶׁר הִתְעוֹרַרְתִּי, שׁוּב הָלַכְתִּי וְהֶחֱלַפְתִּי.
שִׁשִּׁים רִבּוֹא.
שִׁשִּׁים רִבּוֹא.
שִׁשִּׁים רִבּוֹא.

בַּחֲמִימוּת הָעֲמִידָה וְהָאָדָם, חָלַמְתִּי: כַּמָּה הָיָה גֶּשֶׁם.

I walked like a horse

I walked in the rain,
like a myriad of horses.
On one button
a myriad of rain.

On the branches in the square and the avenue walked the rain.
I got tired.
I changed foot after foot
and fell asleep standing.

Until I woke up, again I walked and changed.
Sixty myriad.
Sixty myriad.
Sixty myriad.

In the warmth of the standing and the steam I dreamt: how much
 there was rain.

שומעים את הנהר שלו

אֶרֶץ לָמָּה נָתַתְּ לוֹ אֶת הַקְּבוּרָה.
הֲרֵינִי עוֹמֵד וְזוֹכֵר אֶת הַנָּהָר שֶׁלּוֹ.
וּמֵרָחוֹק שׁוֹמְעִים אֶת הַנָּהָר שֶׁלּוֹ
עִם בַּעַל הַכֶּסֶף הַלָּבָן.

אֵיךְ נְתַתֶּם לוֹ אֶת הַקְּבוּרָה
מִבְּלִי לְהַבִּיעַ אֶת דַּעְתּוֹ בַּנָּדוֹן
מִלִּפְנֵי אָדוֹן חוֹלֵי אָרֶץ.
מְכִילָה אֶרֶץ אֶת הָאָרוֹן.

אֶרֶץ לָמָּה נָתַתְּ לוֹ אֶת הַקְּבוּרָה.
מִפְּנֵי אֲצִילוּת לֹא הִתְעוֹרֵר.
קָרְאוּ דַּוְקָא קָרְאוּ. וְלֹא שָׁבָה הַבְּרָה.
וּבֵית חוֹלִים לֹא מַחֲזֵה אָח שֶׁל מָוֶת.

פֹּה מַשְׁתִּלָה. הַרְכָּבַת גֶּשֶׁר מִן הַבָּרִיא
אֶל הַבָּרִיא. קוֹפְצִים עַל הַמַּכָּה.
מַעֲבִירִים אֶת הַמֹּהַל. בּוֹרְחִים אֶת הָעֲנָפִים.
חוֹתְכִים. חוֹבְרִים. גּוֹזְרִים. גּוֹזְמִים.

הוּא דִּבֵּר בְּשִׁירָה סִפְרוּתִית.
הוּא דִּבֵּר בְּשִׁירָה מְדֻבֶּרֶת:
– אֶת הַתְּחוּם אֵלַי לֹא תַּעֲבֹר.
עַד הַתְּחוּם.

אַתָּה יָפֶה כְּמוֹ גְרֵוְיוּר.
אַתָּה צָרִיךְ לְאַבֵּד עַצְמְךָ לָדַעַת.
– אֵינֶנִּי מֵבִין לִהְיוֹת אוֹ לֹא לִהְיוֹת.
– עוֹד תָּבִין.

40

We hear his river

Earth why did you give him burial.
I am standing and remember his river.
And from a distance we hear his river
with the possessor of the white silver.

How did you give him burial
without consulting his opinion on the matter.
Before the Master earth trembles.
Earth contains the casket.

Earth why did you give him burial.
Because of nobility he didn't wake.
They called indeed they called. And consciousness didn't return.
And hospital is not a play brother of death.

Here a nursery. Assembling a bridge from the healthy
to the healthy. You jump to the blow.
You transfer the sap. You lop the branches.
You cut. You join. You trim. You prune.

He spoke in a literary poetry.
He spoke in a spoken poetry:
—The boundary to me you shall not pass.
Unto the boundary.

You're beautiful like a gravure.
You have to lose yourself to know.*
—I don't understand to be or not to be.
—You'll understand.

---

*The literal rendering of the Hebrew idiom, "to commit suicide."

נא לא לשאול

אִשָּׁה אֲשֶׁר עֲזָבוּהָ
לֹא תֵּלֵךְ עִם טַעֲנוֹת
עַל אֲשֶׁר עֲזָבוּהָ.
הִיא תִּשָּׁכַח בֵּין שִׂיחִים תֵּלֵךְ.
שִׂמְלָתָהּ אֲרֻכָּה עַל יָחֵף.
לֹא רוֹאִים אֶת סַף הָרַגְלַיִם.
אַךְ הַבְּהוֹנוֹת מִסְתַּבְּכוֹת בְּשׁוּלֶיהָ
כְּדָיִג מִתַּחַת הַמַּיִם.

"מִי דּוֹדֵךְ, שׁוּלָה,
שׁוּלַמִּית שׁוּלָה, מִי
דּוֹדֵךְ, אִשָּׁה לֹא
מְבַקֶּשֶׁת, עוֹבֶרֶת, מִי
דּוֹדֵךְ, אֵשֶׁת חַיִל
מִי יִמְצָא, רָחוֹק
מִפְּנִינִים מִכְרָהּ, מִי
דּוֹדֵךְ?" "אַל תְּדַבֵּר."

PLEASE DON'T ASK

A woman who was deserted
won't go about complaining
that she was deserted.
She'll forget among scrub she'll go.
Her dress long over barefoot.
You can't see the edge of her feet.
But the big toes tangle at her hem
like a fisherman under water.

"Who's your truelove, Shula,
Shulamith, Shula, who
is your truelove, unwanted
woman, passing, who
is your truelove, valiant woman
who will find, farther
than pearls her worth, who
is your truelove?" "Don't speak."

אֶת בְּנִי בְּנִי הִדַּחְתִּי
אֶל הָרְחוֹב.
אֶל הָרְחוֹב בְּנִי הִדַּחְתִּי
בְּנִי בְּנִי.
יָצָאתִי הַחוּצָה
קָרָאתִי
בְּנִי בְּנִי יָקָר לִי
בְּנִי.

יָצָא בְּנִי מֵהַמִּסְעָדָה,
זְגוּגִיּוֹת רַבּוֹת מְזַגְּגֶת,
וּבִפְנִים אֲנָשִׁים רַבִּים
יוֹשְׁבִים עִם הָאָב.
"–יָצָאתִי לוֹמַר הִדִּיחַ
הָאָב."

יָצָא בְּנִי מֵהַמִּסְעָדָה:
"–בִּקַּשְׁתִּי מְרַק יְרָקוֹת.
עַכְשָׁו מְבִיאִים הַמָּרָק.
סְלַח לִי."

My son my son I exiled
to the street.
To the street my son I exiled
my son my son.
I went outside
I cried
my son my son is dear to me
my son.

My son left the restaurant,
many windowpanes glazed,
and inside many people
sitting with the back.
"—I left to say exiled
the father."

My son left the restaurant:
"—I asked for vegetable soup.
Now they are bringing the soup.
Excuse me."

אֲנִי אוֹמֵר שָׁלוֹם
וַאֲנִי שׁוֹמֵעַ:
עֵינֵי אָבִיךְ שְׁתֵּי זְכוּכִית
בֵּין שְׁאָר חֲתִיכוֹת פַּח.
גֶּשֶׁם נוֹצֵץ בְּעֵינֵי אָבִיךְ
זוֹ בְּכָה וְזוֹ בְּכָה.

שׁוּב אֲנִי אוֹמֵר
וּפִתְאֹם אֲנִי שׁוֹמֵעַ:
הֲלֹא גַּם אַתָּה
אֶת אָבִיךְ הִדַּחְתָּ.
כְּמוֹ בֵן אֶת אָבִיךְ.
פְּלוֹנִי בֶּן פְּלוֹנִי מִפּוֹלִין.

אֲנִי אוֹמֵר שָׁלוֹם שָׁלוֹם
וְעוֹד אֲנִי אוֹמֵר:
לִפְנֵי שֶׁהָלְכוּ הַשָּׁמַיִם הַשָּׁמַיְמָה,
וְאַתֶּם הַתִּיקִים הַנְּיָרוֹת הַתְּעוּדוֹת,
הִכִּירוּ אוֹתִי כָּל הַזְּמַן הַיֶּלֶד.
עַכְשָׁו אֲנִי שׁוֹמֵעַ בַּפְּרוֹזְדוֹר:"בֵּית הַמִּשְׁפָּט!"

אוֹמְרִים כִּי הַחֲזִיר
הוּא הֲכִי עָשִׁיר.
אוֹכֵל אֶת הַכֹּל.
אֲפִלּוּ זְכוּכִית.
חֲזִיר גָּדוֹל הָאֲדָמָה.
"בֵּית הַמִּשְׁפָּט!"

I say hello
and I hear:
Your father's eyes are two glass
among other bits of tin.
Rain sparkles in your father's eyes
one this wise and one that wise.

Again I say
and suddenly I hear:
Didn't you too
exile your father.
Likewise your father.
So-and-so of so-and-so from Poland.

I say hello hello
and I say more:
Before the skies went skyward,
and with them the files the papers the documents,
they mentioned me all the time the boy.
Now I hear in the corridor: "Law Court!"

They say the pig
is richest.
Eats everything.
Even glass.
A big pig the earth.
"Law Court!"

פְּקָלָאוֹת

שיר מתל אביב

חֲתִיכַת אֶבֶן כִּרְכָּר
נִשְׁבְּרָה מִן הָעִיר.
וַעֲשׂוּיָה מִן הַכִּרְכָּר
מָתַי שְׁאוֹתָהּ הָעִיר.

מֵאָז בִּרְחוֹב בָּרְנֶט,
עִם לִיבְּרַךְ בַּחֶדֶר.
מִשָּׁם לִשְׁכוּ׳ בָּרְנֶר,
עִם מִכְתָּבִים בַּחֶדֶר.

מִשָּׁם לְיִצְחָק אֶלְחָנָן,
עִם שַׁחַט בַּחֶדֶר.
אֵיפֹה שָׁם שַׁחַר־מוֹרְגֶנְשְׁטֶרְן,
שָׁם תַּפּוּחֵי־אַפְּלְבּוֹים בַּחֶדֶר.

מִשָּׁם לִרְחוֹב בּוֹגְרַשׁוֹב, עִם הַפְּקָלָאוֹת.
שָׁם חָלִיתִי שָׁם תָּלִיתִי אֶת הַתְּפִלִּין.
מִשָּׁם הִשְׁלִיכוּ לִי אֶת הַמִּטַּלְטְלִין,
לִפְנֵי שֶׁעוֹד חָזַרְתִּי מִבֵּית חוֹלִים.

מִשָּׁם לִרְחוֹב בּוֹגְרַשׁוֹב.
מִשָּׁם לְשׁוּק הַכַּרְמֶל.
מִשָּׁם לִשְׁכוּ׳ אַבּוּ־כַּדֶּרָה.
מִשָּׁם לִשְׁכוּ׳ שַׁפִּירָא.

מִשָּׁם לִירוּשָׁלַיִם.
מִשָּׁם שׁוּרָה שְׁבִיעִי מִלְמַטָּה.
אֶבֶן הָאֶמְצַע הַמְּעֻכָּה.
הָאַף הַשָּׁבוּר שֶׁל קִיר הַכֹּתֶל.

PACKAGES

Poem from Tel Aviv

A piece of limestone
broke off from the city.
And made from the limestone
when the same city.

Formerly on Barnett Street,
with Librach in the room.
From there to Brenner Quarter,
with letters in the room.

From there to Yitzchak Elchanan,
with Shochat in the room.
Where there's Shachar-Morgenstern,
there Tapuchi-Eppelboim is in the room.

From there to Bograshov, with the packages.
There I got sick there I strung up the *tfillin*.
From there they threw me the movables,
before I even returned from hospital.

From there to Bograshov Street.
From there to Carmel Market.
From there to Abu-Chadra Quar'.
From there to Shapira Quar'.

From there to Jerusalem.
From there seventh row from the bottom.
The crushed middle stone.
The broken nose from The Wall wall.

מִשָּׁם לִירוּשָׁלַיִם.
מִשָּׁם אֶל הַחוֹלוֹת.
שָׁם מָצָאתִי אֶת הַגְּמַלִּים עוֹמְדִים.
בַּשִּׁירָה צְרִיכִים לְהִשְׁתַּמֵּשׁ בְּכֹחַ.

מִשָּׁם לִירוּשָׁלַיִם.
מִשָּׁם לַעֲטָרוֹת.
מִשְׁנַת עֶשְׂרִים וָתֵשַׁע
אֲנִי רֹבֶה קַשָּׁת.

מִשָּׁם לִירוּשָׁלַיִם.
מִשָּׁם לַעֲטָרוֹת.
אֲנִי רֹבֶה קַשָּׁת:
בַּשִּׁירָה צְרִיכִים לָלֶכֶת בְּכֹחַ.

מִשָּׁם לְמַגְדִּיאֵל. לָאָדוֹן בְּיַאלִיק.
לְהַרְאוֹת דֶּרֶךְ מַבְכִּירָה שֶׁלּוֹ.
אַךְ רַק אָחַזְתִּי בַּחֶבֶל,
דָּהֲרָה לְבַדָּהּ אֶל הַשּׁוֹר.

מִשָּׁם לְמַגְדִּיאֵל. לָאָדוֹן וולוֹדְיָה.
לִכְרוֹת קֶבֶר לְאַבָּא שֶׁלּוֹ.
חָצַבְנוּ נָזַז, אֲנִי וְלִיפְשִׁיץ.
בָּא וולוֹדְקָא בָּא: אָבִיו לֹא בָּא.

מִשָּׁם לְמַגְדִּיאֵל. מִמַּגְדִּיאֵל
לִכְפַר-סַבָּא. מִכְּפַר-סַבָּא
לְמִקְוֵה-יִשְׂרָאֵל. מִמִּקְוֵה
לְרִאשׁוֹן-לְצִיּוֹן. מֵרִאשׁוֹן

לִשְׁמִירָה בַּכְּרָמִים, בַּעֲיוּן-קָרָא.
עִם שׁוֹמֵר מִ"נַהֲגֵי הַפְּרָדוֹת", בַּכֶּרֶם.
פַּעַם צִרְעָה עֲקָצַתְהוּ.
קִבֵּל מֶדַלְיָה בְּעַד צִרְעָתְהוּ.

מִשָּׁם לִשְׁכוּ׳ מַחְלוּל.
מִשָּׁם לִשְׁכוּ׳ שַׁפָּאק.
שָׁם עָתִיד הַבְּרָךְ.
שָׁם עָתִיד עַכְשָׁו.

From there to Jerusalem.
From there to the sand dunes.
There I found the camels standing.
In poetry you must use force.

From there to Jerusalem.
From there to Ataroth.
From the year twenty-seven
I am a bowman.

From there to Jerusalem.
From there to Ataroth.
I am a bowman.
In poetry you must go with force.

From there to Magdiel. To Mister Bialik.
To show his primiparous way.
But I only held the rope,
She galloped alone to the ox.

From there to Magdiel. To Mister Volodia.
To dig a grave for his father.
We quarried soilless clay, me and Lifshitz.
Volodka came: his father didn't come.

From there to Magdiel. From Magdiel
to Kfar Saba. From Kfar Saba
to Mikveh Yisrael. From Mikveh
to Rishon le-Tziyon. From Rishon

to watchman work in vineyards, in Ayun-Kara.
With a watchman from "The Mule Drivers," in the vineyard.
Once a wasp didst sting him.
Received a medal for his wasping.

From there to Machlul Quar'.
From there to Shpaak Quar'.
There the city's future.
There the future now.

מִשָּׁם לְשִׁכּוּן מַחְלוּל.
מִשָּׁם לְשִׁכּוּן שַׁפַּאק.
בְּחִפּוּשׂ אַחַר הַבַּיִת.
אַבָּא שֶׁל פַּעַם.

מִשָּׁם לְשִׁכּוּן מַחְלוּל.
מִשָּׁם לְשִׁכּוּן שַׁפַּאק.
שָׁם בַּיִת מְבֻדָּד.
אִישׁ לֹא בָּא לְשָׁם.

שָׁם בַּיִת מְבֻדָּד.
לֹא הוֹלְכִים לְשַׁפַּאק.
עֲשׂוּי קְרָשִׁים וָצֵל.
בְּתֵל אָבִיב תַּלְאוּבָה.

בְּיוֹם שִׁשִּׁי בָּעֶרֶב,
בְּלִי נֵרוֹת.
הִצִּיגוּ סֶרֶט
"פָּרָשׁ בְּלִי רֹאשׁ".

מִשָּׁם נִפְרָדִים. אִישׁ אָמַר,
שֶׁשָּׁם בִּגְרוֹנוֹ עוֹרֵג מַשֶּׁהוּ
מִן הַבַּיִת, שָׁלוֹם. שָׁבוּעַ בָּא
יִהְיֶה לְךָ זוּג נַעֲלַיִם.

שיר ערש לשכונת נורדיה

הַבֶּדוּאִים שֶׁבָּאוּ מִפּוֹלַנְיָה שֶׁלֹּא
כַּמִּתְכֻּנָּן הִתְפַּשְּׁטוּ עַל רְחוֹב
בַּלְפוּר מוּל אֹהֶל שֵׁם עַכְשָׁו וְעַל
הַמִּדְרוֹן מוּל הַשְּׁקֵמִים עַכְשָׁו נוֹרְדִיָּה.

וְהָיוּ בְּאֹהָלִים וְהָיוּ בְּסֻכּוֹת וְהָיוּ בִּצְרִיפִים.
וִידִידַת שֶׁל דֶּלֶת בְּרֹחַב דֶּלֶת וְגָנוֹת.
וְגָנוֹת דָּאוּ בִּילָדִים וְהִשְׁתַּנּוּ.
וְקַיִץ וָחֹרֶף בִּרְחוֹב דִּיזֶנְגּוֹף.

From there to Machlul Quar'.
From there to Shpaak Quar'.
In search of the house.
Father of once.

From there to Machlul Quar'.
From there to Shpaak Quar'.
There a secluded house.
Nobody came there.

There a secluded house.
They don't go to Shpaak.
Made of boards and shade.
In Tel Aviv the scorching.

On Friday eve,
without candles.
They showed a film
The Headless Horseman.

From there we part. Someone said,
that also in his throat yearns something
from home, shalom. Coming week
you'll have a pair of shoes.

Lullaby for Nordia Quarter

The Bedouins who came from Poland not
as planned spread out over Balfour
Street opposite Ohel Shem now and on
the slope opposite the sycamores now Nordia.

And they were in tents and they were in huts and they were in shacks.
And a door handle about the width of a door and roofs.
And roofs glided like children and changed.
And summer and winter on Dizengoff Street.

וּמִסָּבִיב קָמוּ רוֹזְנֵי בָתִּים,
וְהִתְפַּשְּׁטוּ אַרְזֵי בַיִת עַל הַצְּרִיפִים.
תֵּל אָבִיב עִיר הַקֹּדֶשׁ, אֵין לָךְ
שִׁיר עֶרֶשׂ. אֶתְמוֹל זֶה הָיָה.

הָלַכְתִּי בָךְ הַכֹּל בָּרֶגֶל,
כְּמוֹ שֶׁהַסּוּס אוֹכֵל יָשָׁר מֵהָאֲדָמָה.
לִפְעָמִים אֲנִי מוֹסֵר נֶפֶשׁ
בְּעַד כָּל בֶּרֶז שֶׁשָּׁכַחְתִּי פָתוּחַ.

הָלַכְתִּי בָךְ בָּעֲזָרָה שֶׁעָזַבְתִּי.
בָּעִיר שֶׁלָּךְ, בַּעֲזָרָה שֶׁלִּי.
אֶת הָעֲזָרָה שֶׁלִּי שֶׁמֵּאֲחוֹרֵי גַּבֵּךְ
וְאֶת עַצְמִי אֲנִי, כְּלַפַּיִךְ זָרַקְתִּי.

הָלַכְתִּי בָךְ הַכֹּל.
רֵאשִׁית כֹּל נֶחֱרַב בַּיִת רִאשׁוֹן.
שֵׁנִית כֹּל נֶחֱרַב בַּיִת שֵׁנִי:
בָּא בּוּלְדּוֹזֶר בָּעַט בַּבַּיִת.

דְּזַבִּין אַבָּא חֲבֵרִים.
יוֹם אֶחָד אֲנִי שָׂם יָדִי עַל כְּתֵפוֹ,
וְהוּא יָדוֹ עַל יְרֵכֵךְ.
כָּךְ יוֹצְאִים כָּל חֲבֵרַיִךְ.

וּבָעִיר אֵין לִי לְוָיוֹת אֶלָּא שֶׁל
אַחַד הָעָם, בְּיַאלִיק, נוֹרְדוֹי, שֶׁמְּמַשֵּׁךְ
אֶת שְׁמוֹ עַל הַשְּׁכוּנָה עַל שְׁמוֹ
שֶׁמַּעֲבֶכֶת אֶת נוֹרְדִיָּה כִּמְרוֹם אֲשֶׁךְ.

And all about rose up baronic houses.
And domestic cedar spread out over the shacks.
Tel Aviv holy city, you have no
lullaby. Yesterday that was.

I walked in you everything by foot,
like the horse eats straight from the earth.
There are times I suffer martyrdom
for every faucet you forgot open.

I walked in you in the town I left.
In your city, in my town.
My city that's behind your back
and myself me, toward you I heft.

I walked in you everything.
Firstly was destroyed the first house.
Secondly was destroyed the second house:
came a bulldozer kicked at the house.

"As Father bought" friends.
One day I'm there my hand on his shoulder,
and he his hand on your thigh.
So exit all your friends.

And in the city I've no funerals except of
Achad Ha-Am, Bialik, Nordau, who drew
his name on the quarter on his name
for you crushed Nordia as you bruise a testicle.

שלושה שירי ילדות

שיר מס' אחת

בִּימֵי קְטֹף כַּלָּנִיּוֹת בַּשָּׁרוֹנָה.
וַיְהִי בִּשְׂדֵה כַּלָּנִיּוֹת בַּשָּׁרוֹנָה,
הָלְכָה יַלְדָּה וְקִטְפָה.
הָלְכָה רוּחַ וְחָטְפָה

עָלֶה אַחַר עָלֶה,
כָּל הַפֶּרַח כָּלֶה.
נִשְׁאַר לָהּ קְנוֹקֶנֶת.
הָלְכָה עִם זֶה.

שיר מס' שתיים

בֵּית סֵפֶר שֶׁל גּוֹרְדּוֹן בַּשָּׁרוֹנָה לִרְכִיבָה עַל סוּסִים.
וְאִלּוּ גּוֹרְדּוֹן פְּנֵי גָּמָל.
הָאַף שֶׁלּוֹ מְקֻפָּל אֶצְלִי בַּנְּיָר
וַאֲנִי מַחֲזִיק אוֹתוֹ בַּכִּיס מְכוֹפָף.

צְבָרִים אַדִּירִים בִּקְלִפּוֹת, פְּנֵי גּוֹרְדּוֹן.
הֶעָלִים הַפִּשְׁתָּן הִתִּירַס, פְּנֵי גּוֹרְדּוֹן.
תָּלִישׁ וְקַלָּח וּכְרוּב פֶּרַח, פְּנֵי גּוֹרְדּוֹן.
גָּמָל הוֹלֵךְ. אַלְמָה. לֶקֶט. שִׁכְחָה. פְּנֵי גּוֹרְדּוֹן.

וְהַסּוּס פֶּטֶר הוּא אֵבֶר כְּכָנָף.
גָּדוֹל בִּרְכִיבָה הוּא לְעֵינֶיהָ.
הַגָּמָל הוּא אַלְמָה שֶׁל שֶׁקֶט וְשֶׁל שִׁכְחָה.
וְהַסּוּס פֶּטֶר הוּא גָּדוֹל.

THREE LITTLE-GIRL POEMS

Poem no. one

In anemone-plucking time in Sharona.
And it came to pass in an anemone field in Sharona,
a girl walked and plucked.
A wind walked and snatched

petal after petal,
all the flower dismantled.
She was left with stem.
She walked with them.

Poem no. two

The Gordon School in Sharona for horseback riding.
Whereas Gordon had a camel face.
His nose is with me folded in paper
and I keep it in my pocket bent.

Mighty prickly pear in husk, Gordon's face.
The leaves the flax the corn, Gordon's face.
Pluck and stalk and flower cabbage, Gordon's face.
A camel walks. Sheaf. Gleaning. Forgetfulness. Gordon's face.

And the horse Peter is a limb. Like a wing.
Big in riding he is in her eyes.
The camel is a sheaf of silence and of forgetfulness.
And the horse Peter is big.

שיר מס׳ שלוש

אִישׁ אֵינֶנּוּ. אִשָּׁה
מְחַלֶּקֶת שְׂמָלוֹת, מִמְחָטוֹת,
לְנַעֲרוֹת דּוֹדָתָהּ.
זוֹרֶקֶת אֵל עַל אֶת הַשּׁוֹרְטְס.

הַקִּירוֹת הִזְעִיקוּ שְׁתִיקָה.
הַחַלּוֹנוֹת הֶחֱזִירוּ חֲלוֹף עַיִן לָרְחוֹב.
כִּי הוֹלֶכֶת מִכָּאן. כִּי הֶחֱזִירָה לְאִמָּהּ
אֶת סַכִּין הַלֶּחֶם.

הַחֲתוּלָה לֹא עוֹזֶבֶת אֶת אַרְגַּז הַמַּצָּע
הָרֵיק.
הֵרִיחָה אֶת הַכְּבָסִים מִבִּפְנִים שֶׁבַּחוּץ,
וַתְּיַלֵּל.

Poem no. three

No one around. A woman
distributes dresses, handkerchiefs,
to her aunt's girls.
Tosses on high the shorts.

The walls warned silence.
The windows returned an ephemeral eye to the street.
Because she's off. Because she returned the bread knife
to her mother.

The kitten won't leave the empty box
bed.
She smelled the washing from inside that's out,
and yowwwled.

שבעה על הגשם

אחד

הַשָּׁמַיִם הִצִּילוּ מִילְיוֹן
דּוּנָם תְּבוּאוֹת.
מֶזֶג הָאֲוִיר הַגָּשׁוּם וְהַסּוֹ־
עֵר שֶׁשָּׂרַר אֶתְמוֹל בָּרֹב

חֶלְקֵי הָאָרֶץ נִתְקַבֵּל בְּבִרְ־
כָה וּבְסִפּוּק עַל יְדֵי הַחַקְלָ־
אִים. יַחַד עִם זֹאת גָּרְמוּ
הַגְּשָׁמִים לִקְשָׁיִים בַּתַּחְבּוּרָה

בִּמְקוֹמוֹת שׁוֹנִים וְלַהֲצָפַת
רְחוֹבוֹת וּבָתִּים
בְּכַמָּה עָרִים. הַצֶּמַח מֵאֲחוֹרֵי
קִיר שׁוֹמֵעַ.

שניים

הַצֶּמַח הֻכְנַס לַחֶדֶר
בְּיוֹם ב בָּעֶרֶב.
אֶת מֵימָיו הוּא מְקַבֵּל
מִן הַמַּיִם שֶׁלָּנוּ.

מֵאֲחוֹרֵי הַקִּיר
שׁוֹמֵעַ רַעַם.
עוֹמֵד בַּגֶּשֶׁם
לְפִי הַשְּׁמוּעָה.

גֶּשֶׁם הַפְּתִיחָה.
גֶּשֶׁם הַגְּלִילָה.
גֶּשֶׁם הַזְּלִיפָה.
גֶּשֶׁם הַחֲלִיבָה.

SEVEN ON THE RAIN

One

The rains saved a million
dunam crops.
The rainy and stormy wea-
ther which prevailed yesterday in most

parts of the land was received with heart-
y approval by the far-
mers. At the same time the rains
caused difficulties in transportation

in several areas and the flooding of
roads and houses
in a few cities. The plant behind
wall hears.

Two

The plant was brought in the room
on Monday evening.
Its water it receives
from our water.

Behind the wall
hears thunder.
Stands in the rain
goes the rumor.

The opening rain.
The rolling rain.
The spraying rain.
The milking rain.

שלושה

גֶּשֶׁם הַפְּתִיחָה
מִתְעַטְּפִים בַּחוּץ בְּטַלֵּיתִים
כְּבְלֵיל כָּל נִדְרֵי.
הֶעָלִים בַּחוּץ וְהַיְלָדִים בַּחוּץ
וְרִשְׁרוּשׁ וְרַשְׁרַעַשׁ וַאֲסֵפַת סוּפוֹת.
הַחַיִּים עוֹבְרִים וְגַם הַמָּוֶת עוֹבֵר
וְגַם שְׁאֵלוֹת הַשְּׂרוּפוֹת.

גֶּשֶׁם הַגָּלִילָה
בְּנִגְמַר יוֹם הַשּׁוּק
עוֹד יוֹתֵר נוּגֶה.
גּוֹלְלִים אֵיזֶה קֶלַף. מוֹלְלִים אֵיזֶה מַטְבְּעוֹת.
כַּמָּה יֵשׁ שְׂחוֹקִים. שְׁווּקִים. שְׂרוּקִים.

גֶּשֶׁם הַזְּלִיפָה
כְּבְלֵיל כָּל נִדְרֵי.
זְלִיפַת עֲטִינִים
לְתוֹךְ הַדְּלִי דְּלָלָל.
וְכֵן הַחֲלִיבָה.

ארבעה

רִבּוֹנוֹ שֶׁל
שָׁמַיִם,
אַיֵּה
יוֹנֵי הַבָּר?

בְּגֶשֶׁם נִמְלְטָה
כַּלְבָּה בְּשֵׁם
דִּבָּה לְהֵיכַל
הַשַּׁמֶּשֶׁת.

Three

The opening rain
they wrap outside in *talleisim*
as on Kol Nidrei eve.
The leaves outside and the children outside
rustle blustle and a mustering of storms.
Life passes and also death passes
also the burned questions.

The rolling rain
at the close of a market day
even more gloomy.
They roll some parchment. Rub some coins.
How many are there bruised. Bartered. Battlemented.

The spraying rain
as on Kol Nidrei eve.
Spraying cow-teat
into the pail plll.
And so the milking.

Four

Lord of
heaven,
where are
the wild doves?

In the rain scampered off
a bitch named
Dooba to the Palace
of Shamash.

צַמְרוֹת גֶּשֶׁם
פָּרְצוּ אַחֲרֵי
עָלֶה שֶׁעוֹד
יָרֹק נָשַׁר.

גֶּשֶׁם בִּשְׁלֶכֶת
הוּחַל בָּאֲזַדְרֶכֶת.
וְלֹא יְלוּדֵי נָשִׁים,
כִּי יְלוּדֵי יוֹנִים,

קַן תְּפִלּוֹתֵיהֶן
וְדִבְיוֹנֵיהֶן,
עֲשׂוּ לָהֶן
קְצָת בַּיִת.

עֲשׂוּ לָהֶן
קְצָת בֵּעָיוֹת
הַקִּנִּים הַקְּרֵחִים
שֶׁל יוֹנֵי הַבָּר.

כְּמוֹ שֶׁסּוֹכְכִים
בְּדַם הַשּׁוֹשַׁנִּים
עֲשׂוּ לָךְ,
שְׁכוּנַת נוֹרְדִיָּה.

מִקְצוֹת הָעֲנָפִים
הַנְּמוּכִים
הָרוּחַ הִגִּירָתַם
וְהַגֶּשֶׁם טְרַדְרַד.

רִבּוֹנוֹ שֶׁל שָׁמַיִם,
אַיֵּה יוֹנֵי הַבָּר?
הֵיכָן תַּחְבִּיאָן?
שֶׁל כְּנָפֶיךָ.

נִשְׁמַעַת נְזִלַת.
פַּעַם כֵּן פַּעַם לֹא.
וּפַעַם כֵּן כֵּן.
וְהַפְסָקָה.

Echelons of rain
rushed upon
a leaf that still
green fell.

Rain in Fall
whirled in the margosa tree.
And not women-bred,
but dove-bred,

nest of their prayers
and their dove-dung,
made them
a bit of home.

Made them
a bit of a problem
the bald lice
of the wild doves.

Like agents
in rose blood
did to you
Nordia Quarter.

From the tips of the low
branches
the wind migrated 'em
the rain harrrasssed.

Lord of heaven,
where are the wild doves?
Where didst you hide them?
Fault of thy wings.

A drip is heard.
Once yes once no.
And once yes yes.
Then a break.

הַדַּרְן אוֹמֵר
הַקְרִין, וּמוֹדִיעַ.
וּבְאוֹתוֹ רֶגַע –
חֲלַאף.

תַּקְרִית שָׁמַיִם
עַל הַסַּף.
הַבֹּל נִשְׁפָּךְ.
וְכֵן הַשַּׁק.

חמשה

אַתָּה גֶּשֶׁם מְשֻׁנֶּה
גַּג הָאֲדָמָה.
מְזַגְזֵג
דַּרְכְּךָ

לִמְקוֹמוֹת נְמוּכִים
בָּאֲדָמָה. לֹא
לַעֲלוֹת וְלֹא
לָרֶדֶת. שׁוֹלֵחַ

שַׁלְשָׁלִים בַּעֲלֵי
טֶבַע רַכָּה.
מַהֵר יוֹתֵר,
נָמוּךְ יוֹתֵר.

אַתָּה טֶבַע
לֹא מִבַּיִת.
אוֹמֵר
בְּפַחֵי מַיִם

לְחַפֵּשׂ בִּמְקוֹמוֹת
נְמוּכִים מֶחְלָה
בָּאֲדָמָה. הַמַּרְטִיב
עַד מֹחַ. וְלֹא

I repeat says
the announcer, and reports.
And at the same time—
thwaak.

A sky incident
on the threshold.
Everything spilled.
Likewise the sack.

Five

You, rain, alter
earth's roof.
Zigzagging
your way

to low places
in the earth. Not
to go up nor
to come down. Sending

tree worms of
soft nature.
Faster,
lower.

You are nature
not inside.
Standing
in water tanks

to search out in low
places burrows
in the earth. Wetting
to the brain. Nor

נוֹתֵן מָנוֹחַ
לְהִתְיַבֵּשׁ. לִפְעָמִים
חוֹמֶק כְּמַקָּק
מִקִּיר. וְלִפְעָמִים

הֵם עוֹלִים כֻּלָּם
עַל הַכִּרְכָּרָה דְּחוּקִים וּדְחוּפִים
וְעוֹלִים מַהֵר וְלִנְסֹעַ וְנוֹסְעִים
מַהֵר מַהֵר מִכָּאן.

ששה

אֵינֶנִּי פוֹגֵשׁ אֲנָשִׁים
שֶׁל שֶׁלִּי – שֶׁלִּי.
שׁוֹמֵעַ רְעָמִים מֻפְשָׁטִים בּוֹדְדִים
תַּחַת הַשָּׁמַיִם.

יִבַּשְׁתִּי אֶת הֶעָצִיץ הַגָּדוֹל מֵאֲדָמָה.
וְשָׁמַעְתִּי אֶת הַטִּפּוֹת לְהִדּוֹבֵב.
וְנָקַשְׁתִּי בְּיָד בֶּעָצִיץ.
הֲשָׁלֵם לֶעָצִיץ. וַיֹּאמֶר שָׁלֵם.

אוֹצָר אֵין בָּאֲדָמָה.
וְאִם יֵשׁ, הוּא
אֲשֶׁר יָצַר.
אֲשֶׁר אָמַר קָדָר:

מַיִם זֶה צֶמַח הַמִּדְבָּר.
מַה לַּמַּיִם בֵּין בְּנֵי אָדָם?
מַיִם בָּאוּ וְיָצְאוּ,
מַיִם בָּאוּ וְיָצְאוּ.

קָדַחְתִּי נְקָרָה בַּתַּחְתִּית
לְמוֹצָאֵי מַיִם.
גֶּשֶׁם גֶּשֶׁם בָּא.
מַיִם בָּאִים וְיוֹצְאִים.

letting up
to dry. Sometimes
absconding like a bookworm
from a wall. And sometimes

they all pile
in a carriage packed and pressing
pile in fast and for to travel and they travel
fast fast from here.

Six

I don't meet my kind
of people — my kind.
I hear vague broken thunder
under the sky.

I dried the big flowerpot of earth.
And heard the drops moved to whisper.
And kissed the flowerpot with my hand.
All intact with flowerpot? It said intact.

No treasure house in earth.
And if there is, it's He
who created.
Who potter said:

water is the desert plant.
What has water to do with people?
Water came and went,
water came and went.

I drilled a crevice in the bottom
an exit for water.
Rain rain come.
Water comes and goes.

גֶּשֶׁם בָּא לְפִי מִשְׁכָּל.
מַיִם בָּאִים וְיוֹצְאִים.
מַיִם מַיִם בָּאִים.
גֶּשֶׁם בָּא מִתְחַסְכֵּל.

הַגְּשָׁמִים הוֹלִידוּ צְפַרְדֵּעַ. בָּרְחוֹב
קָפְצָה פִּיהָ מְנוֹתַר מַיִם.
מַיִם מַיִם בָּאִים.
מְאוֹתָם מַיִם.

בְּעֵינַי רָאִיתִי עֵגֶל, כִּדְיוּק קָטָן, מְלַקֵּק בְּאַפּוֹ
וּמֵרִיחַ רִתְמַת עוֹר, מִשֶּׁהִגִּיעַ לוֹ זֵכֶר מֵאִמּוֹ.
מִכָּאן רוֹקֶמֶת שְׁחָקִים מְכַסָּה אֶת יַלְדָּהּ,
אֶת אֶמְצַע הַיֶּלֶד בְּאֶמְצַע הַלַּיְלָה.

שבעה

זְרִיקַת אֶבֶן בַּבִּצָּה,
זוֹ מַתָּנָה מֵאֱלֹהִים לְהִתְקַשְּׁרוּת עִם כִּנּוֹר.
יוֹם כִּנּוֹר הוּא יוֹם תְּפִלָּה.
הַתֹּף דּוֹפֵק תְּפִלָּה בְּיוֹם כִּנּוֹר.

הַתֹּף דּוֹפֵק תְּשׁוּבָה בְּיוֹם כִּנּוֹר.
הַתֹּף מְדוֹפְקִי לִתְשׁוּבָה הַתֹּף.
הַתֹּף דּוֹפֵק אֶת עַצְמוֹ
טוֹב. וְהָעָם רוֹאִים אֶת הַכֵּלִים.

Rain comes by concept.
Water comes and goes.
Water water comes.
Rain comes ingeniously.

The rains begat frog. In the street
her mouth leaped with remnant water.
Water water comes.
From the same water.

With my own eyes I saw a calf, like a small roach, licking with its
  muzzle
smelling saddle leather, from which reached it a trace of its mother.
Hence skies stretch out cover a small girl,
the middle of the child in the middle of the night.

Seven

A stone tossed into the mire,
is a gift of God for commitment to lyre.
A lyre day is a day of prayer.
The drum bangs prayer on a lyre day.

The drum bangs repentance on a lyre day.
The drum of repentance-bangers the drum.
The drum bangs himself
good. And the nation sees the instruments.

1 ינואר, לילה

בְּבֵית קָפֶה, מִצַּד הָרְחוֹב.
מִי שֶׁהָיוּ פֹּה – אֵינָם.
מִי שֶׁחָשׁוּב בֶּאֱמֶת
וּמִי שֶׁחָשׁוּב כְּנָם.

רַק סַדְרָן זָקֵן מִן הַקּוֹלְנוֹעַ
עִם לַבְלָר זָקֵן מִן "הַבִּימָה".
וְהַדֻּבָּה הַגְּדוֹלָה עַל הַגַּג
מְצִיצָה אֵלֶיהָ פְּנִימָה.

מְשַׂחֲקִים שָׁח. הַבַּיִת
קָפֶה מָלֵא דֶּצֶמְבֶּר.
שׁוֹמְעִים ג'וֹן בָּאֶז
שָׁרָה אַי רִימֶמְבֶּר.

January 1st, night

In the café, at the side of the street.
He who were here—are gone.
He important as dead
and he important as sleeper.

Just an old usher from the cinema
with an old white from "Habima."
And the Great Bear on the roof
peeps at her in there.

Playing chess. The house
café cram-full December.
Listening to Joan Baez
sing "I remember."

זוטות מתל אביב

רְח׳ נַחֲלַת בִּנְיָמִין
עִם הַצֵּל הַקָּטָן.
וָאדִי נַחַל בִּנְיָמִין
נַעֲשָׂה עַכְשָׁוִי.

וַאֲנִי קוֹשֵׁר זֹאת עִם מ. דִּיזֶנְגוֹף רֹאשׁ עִיר
רוֹכֵב סוּס שֶׁעָבַר בְּנַחֲלַת בִּנְיָמִין
וַאֲנִי קוֹשֵׁר אֶת סְלִיחוֹתַי הַקְּרוּעוֹת
עִם שְׂרוֹכֵי הַנַּעֲלַיִם שֶׁלִּי.

בִּשְׁכוּ׳ בְּרֶנֶר שָׂרַף צָרִיף
גַּפְרוּר הַשֶּׁמֶשׁ. כַּדּוּר הַשֶּׁמֶשׁ
גָּר שָׁם. שְׂכַר דִּירָה
בִּמְעַט וְלֹא. הָעִקָּר שֶׁנִּרְתַּתִּי.

Miniatures from Tel Aviv

Nachalat Binyamin St.
with the little shadow.
Wadi Binyamin River
has become timely.

And I connect this with M. Dizengoff, Mayor
riding a horse now past on Nachalat Binyamin
and I connect my torn soles
with my shoelaces.

In the Brenner Quarter the sun's match
burned a shack. The sun's sphere
lives there. Rent
almost not. Most important I lived.

שירים מקומיים

צמיחה

יֵשׁ דָּבָר הַנִּרְאֶה בַּמּוּזִיקָה צְמִיחָה.
דִּיבֶלוֹפְּמֶנְט. זֹאת אוֹמֶרֶת צְמִיחָה בְּשִׁנּוּי.
בְּחֻקֵּי חֹק תֵּבִי. שׁוֹמְעִים מוּזִיקָה
נַעֲשֶׂה בַּיִת. ז.א. מוּזִיקָה צוֹמַחַת מִן הַהֲרִיסָה.

וְיֵשׁ אֶחָד בַּיָּמִים מִתְהַלֵּךְ
עִם כַּמָּה דְּבָרִים בַּנְּשָׁמָה.
זֶה מְעַנְיֵן אוֹתוֹ? אֲבָל
תָּמִיד עַל הַשֶּׁטַח. לְמָשָׁל

שֶׁטַח שֶׁהָיָה פַּעַם שְׁכוּנַת נוֹרְדִיָּה.
נֶחְשְׂפָה שׁוּרָה שֶׁל בָּתִּים.
בֵּין בַּיִת לְבֵית אֲדָמָה.
כָּל בַּיִת עוֹד מִן הָאֳנִיָּה שָׁקוּעַ.

הֵם נִקְרְאוּ וַעֲלֵיהֶם לָבוֹא.
יְהוּדֵי תֵּל אָבִיב בָּאוּ וְיוֹשְׁבִים
בַּשֶּׁטַח
שְׁכוּ' נוֹרְדִיָּה סָנְטָה קָתָרִינָה בֵּית הַמִּקְדָּשׁ.

סוֹף קַיִץ

עַל הָעֵץ הַיָּבֵשׁ
מְקַנְּחוֹת אֶת הַפֶּה.
וְהָקֵן הֶהָרוּס
בְּצִדֵּי הָעֵץ.

LOCAL POEMS

Growth

There is something that seems in music growth.
"Development." That is, growth in change.
Parrot paraphrase by precept. You hear music
it becomes a house. i.e. music grows from destruction.

And there is one through days goes
with several things in the soul.
It interests him? But
always on the surface. For example

an area once the Nordia Quarter.
A line of houses was stripped.
Between house and house earth.
Each house still from the ship submerged.

They were called and had to come.
The Jews of Tel Aviv came and reside
in the area of
Nordia Quar' Santa Caterina The Temple.

End of summer

On the dry tree
they wipe off the mouth.
And the ruined nest
at the side of the tree.

מוֹךְ שֶׁל צִפֳּרִים
בְּכָל מָקוֹם.
כָּל הַצִפֳּרִים מְרַגְּשׁוֹת מָעוֹן
לָשֶׁבֶת בְּחֹרֶף.

נַעֲלַיִם בְּיָד.
בִּשְׂחִי.
אַרְנֶבֶת
בּוֹרַחַת בְּחֹרֶף.

צִפּוֹר בְּמַקּוֹר
קְצָת פָּתוּחַ.
אִם אֵין רוּחַ
אֵין טִיסָה.

תְּהִלִּים מֶלֶךְ הָעוֹלָם.
אִלּוּ כָּל הַנְּהָרוֹת דְּיוֹ.
אִלּוּ כָּל הַיְּעָרוֹת עֵטִים.
אִלּוּ כָּתַבְתִּי יוֹם וּכְתַבְתִּי לַיְלָה כָּתַבְתִּים.

תֵּן לִי רֶגַע אֶחָד. תֵּן לִי רֶגֶשׁ
לְהוֹצִיא מִן הַפֶּה מִלָּה לֹא נְכוֹנָה.
שֶׁמִּישֶׁהוּ מְדַבֵּר שִׂיחָה שְׁלֵמָה מוֹצִיא
מִן הַפֶּה מִלָּה לֹא נְכוֹנָה לַבַּסּוֹף.

אִלּוּ אֶת כָּל הַיְּעָרוֹת בּוֹרְתִים.
אִלּוּ כָּל הָעֵצִים כּוֹתְבִים.
כָּל הַכּוֹתְבִים רַדְיוֹאַקְטִיבִיִּים
וְכָל הַקּוֹרְאִים שׁוֹרְטִים.

חֲמִשָּׁה עָשָׂר יֵשׁ מִילְיוֹן יְהוּדִים גְּרַאפּוֹמָאנִים
וְסוֹפֵר יֵשׁ אֶחָד.
חֲלָצָה בְּגָרוּשׁ עָלֶיהָ. הֲרִימָה פָּנִים לִרְאוֹת אִם יִהְיֶה גֶּשֶׁם.
וְחוֹזֶרֶת אֶל מְקוֹמָהּ.

קַבָּלוּהָ בְּהִתְיַבְּשׁוּת.
לֹא בְּהִשְׁתַּתְּפוּת.
מַה יֵּשׁ חֲדָשׁוֹת?
אֵין יֵשׁ חֲדָשׁוֹת.

Bird down
all over.
All the birds sensitize a dwelling
to settle in winter.

Shoes in hand.
In armpit.
Rabbit
flees in winter.

Bird at the bill
a bit open.
If there's no wind
no flight.

Psalms—King of the World.
Were all the rivers ink.
Were all the forests pens.
If I writ day and I writ night writs.

Give me a minute. Give me a feeling
to utter a wrong word from the mouth.
That someone giving a whole spiel utters
a wrong word from the mouth at the end.

Were all the forests razed.
Were all the trees writers.
All the writers radioactive
and all the readers scratchers.

Fifteen there are million Jews graphomaniacs.
Writer, there is one.
Penny blouse on her. She lifted her face to see if it would rain.
And returns to her place.

They greeted her with dessication.
Not cooperation.
What's the news?
Not's the news.

מַה יֵּשׁ בַּיַּעַר?
אֲנִי צְרִיכָה זֶה בִּשְׁבִיל הַבַּיִת.
אֵיךְ זֶה נִקְרָא?
יֶרֶק.

עָבְרוּ עָלֶיהָ סוּס עוֹמֵד בַּחֹשֶׁךְ. עָבְרוּ עָלֶיהָ
צְטָרָבָלִים זוֹרְקִים זֵרִים קוֹצִים שׁוֹטִים.
כָּכָה הָעֲבוֹדָה. מִיָּד אַחֲרֵי חֻרְבַּן בֵּית הַמִּקְדָּשׁ הֶחֱלוּ בַּהַשְׁפָּלָה בִּזְרִיקָה
שֶׁל בּוּדְזִיאָקִים – יָשָׁר צְעִירִים בְּזִקְנֵי זְקֵנָם, כְּשׁוֹר נוֹגֵחַ שׁוֹר בִּשְׁרִיקָה.

עָבְרוּ עָלֶיהָ חֲלוֹמוֹת לְפִי קַוֵּי תָּמִיד שֶׁל חֲלוֹמוֹתֶיהָ. סוֹבְבָה
אֲדָמָה בִּשְׁפוּעִים וּבֵצָה עַל שְׂפַת קַרְקַע.
כַּמָּה בֵּצָה כַּמָּה עֹמֶק
לֹא הָיָה אֶת מִי לִשְׁאֹל.

כָּל זֶה אֵינֶנּוּ שַׁיָּךְ לְשִׁירָה.
הַמַּשְׂכִּיל בָּעֵת הַהִיא אַף הוּא לֹא כָּתַב
שְׁנַיִם מִקְרָא וְאֶחָד תַּרְגּוּם לְעַרְבִית.
עַרְבִי יָחִיד בְּ"מֵתֵי מִדְבָּר" דֶּרֶךְ אַגַּב.

בָּנָיו זִילַאנְד צִפּוֹר בְּשֶׁלֶג.
מִתַּחַת הַשֶּׁלֶג מֵימֵי שֶׁלְּנוּ
זוֹחֵל הַקּוֹל הַצִּפּוֹרִי.
וְיוֹנֵי הַבַּר שֶׁלִּי.

עוֹד מְעַט יֵרֵד הַקֵּן
לַעֲבוֹד. הַחֹמֶר מִמֶּנּוּ עָשׂוּי
מָצוּי. הוּכַח מַסְפִּיק אֶפְשָׁר לִבְנוֹת בֵּית מַחְמָר
דָּלִיק. גַּם לְיוֹנֵי בָּר יֵשׁ צֶבַע דָּלִיק.

לֹא יִבְנוּ בַּיִת?
מַה יַּעֲשׂוּ יוֹנֵי בָּר?
לְאָן יוֹלִיכוּ אֶת הַסְּבִיבָה?
וַדַּאי יִבְנוּ בַּיִת.

What's in the forest?
I need it for the house.
How's it called?
Greens.

She underwent a horse standing in darkness. She underwent
pine cones flinging whip thorn garlands.
That's plain fact. Right after the destruction of the Temple began
    humiliation with an injection
of Bodzyakim—straightway youth at the beards of their peers, like ox
    goring ox with a whistle.

She underwent dreams by the constant lines of her dreams. Earth
spun with slopes and mire on land's rim.
How much mire how much depth
there was no one to ask.

All this doesn't belong to poetry.
The enlightened in that age didn't write either
two parts Bible and one part translation into Arabic.
Only one Arab in "Desert Dead" incidentally.

In New Zealand a bird in snow.
Under the snow from my snow days
crawls the birdlike voice.
and my wild doves.

Soon the nest will come down
for processing. The material from which it is made
available. It has been amply proven a house may be built of
    inflammable
material. Wild doves also have an inflammable color.

They won't build house?
What will the wild doves do?
Where will they lead the environment?
Of course they'll build house.

שָׁבוּת

הָיִיתִי שׁוֹמֵר כְּרָמִים
וְיָרַדְתִּי בִּגְמַר הַבָּצִיר מֵהַמְּלוּנָה
מֵהַכֶּרֶם. וְכָל הַשּׁוֹמְרִים עִם הַחֲבִילָה
וְעִם הַכְּסוּת יָרְדוּ מֵהַמְּלוּנָה מֵהַכֶּרֶם.

אֲנִי רוֹאֶה כָּאן אִישׁ
וַחֲבִילָתוֹ בָּא אֶל סַפְסָל
בַּשְּׂדֵרָה. יָשֵׁן אֶת לֵילוֹ
וְהוֹלֵךְ וְלַשְּׂדֵרָה הוּא שָׁב.

עַד שֶׁבָּא סְתָו. מְעִיל
לָבַשׁ נָעַל
אַךְ
אֵין לוֹ מָקוֹם

לִשְׁכַּב עַל סַפְסָל. פְּתוּחוֹת הַנַּעֲלַיִם בַּצַּד
שָׁם הוּא שׁוֹכֵב
עַל קְרָשִׁים אַרְבָּעָה
לִנְשֹׁם עָמֹק.

לִשְׁכַּב עַל סַפְסָל
עַל טָהֳרַת הַקְּרָשִׁים
כִּצְנִפַת הַקֵּן הֶחָשׂוּף
שֶׁבְּצִדֵּי הָעֵץ.

שְׁנֵי צְעָדִים מִכָּאן שׁוֹכֵב הַיָּם
חָלָק בְּתַאֲרִיךְ 8 דֶּצֶמְבֶּר.
וּבָאֹפֶק סָבִיב עַמִּים וּמְדִינוֹת וַעֲנָנִים
וּשְׁתֵּי הַנַּעֲלַיִם פְּתוּחוֹת.

Lull

I was a vineyard watchman
and descended at the end of the vintage from the hut
from the vineyard. And all the watchmen with the bundle
and with the raiment descended from the hut from the vineyard.

I see a man here
and his bundle come to a bench
on the avenue. Sleeps his night
and goes and to the avenue he returns.

Until autumn comes. Coat
he wore shoe
but
has no place

to lie on a bench. The shoes are open on the side
where he lies
on boards four
to breathe deep.

To lie on a bench
on the purity of the boards
like coil of the bared nest
at the side of the tree.

Two steps from here lies the sea
smooth on the date 8 December.
And on the horizon around nations and states and clouds
and the two shoes open.

עֵץ

שְׁאַל אוֹתָהּ אִם זוֹכֶרֶת הִיא אֶת הַקַּיִץ – לֹא.
עֶרֶב שֶׁלָּהּ לְחוּפְשִׁי קֵן מְפֻחָד נְשִׁירַת עָלִים
מֵאַלְמוּת גֶּשֶׁם שֶׁל הַסְּתָו
עַכְשָׁו.

הָאַזְדֶּרֶכֶת בֵּית הַלַּיְלָה שֶׁל הַצֵּל. כִּי הַצֵּל
הוּא הַבַּיִת. בֵּית עוֹלָמִים לְיוֹנֵי בָּר וְעוֹד
בִּנְפֵי קַיִץ. בֵּית עוֹלָמִים שֶׁל גּוּפֵי בָּר
וְחַיּוֹת בָּר עוֹלִים בָּעֵץ. וְעַכְשָׁו אֵין אַף אֶחָד.

אַלִּימוּת הַגֶּשֶׁם מִן הַסְּתָו עַל הַחַלּוֹן.
נוֹפֵל לָהּ גּוֹרָל. נוֹשֵׁר לָהּ נוֹפֵל לָהּ.
לֹא יְכוֹלָה. בִּזְרוֹעוֹת חֲשׂוּפוֹת הִגִּיעָה עַד הַחַלּוֹן.
הַיּוֹרֶה זֶה הַמָּוֶת שֶׁלָּהּ.

נְשִׁירַת עָלִים דּוֹמָה לִנְדִידַת צִפֳּרִים.
בַּחֹרֶף נוֹשֵׁר וּבַקַּיִץ חוֹזֵר. אֲבָל צִפֳּרִים בַּחוּץ
וְעָלִים בִּפְנִים. וּבַמִּקְרֶה שֶׁלְּפָנֵינוּ עָלִים יְכוֹלִים גַּם לֹא לָשׁוּב.
דַּע לְךָ.

מי שבא מן הכוכבים

אַזְדֶּרֶכֶת מִתְחַתֶּוֶת אוֹהֶבֶת אֶת הַסְּתָו.
אֵין לָהּ צַמֶּרֶת וְאֵין לָהּ צְמַרְמֹרֶת.
הֶחֱזִיקָה עוֹד כַּמָּה יָמִים. עָלִים סְדוּקִים וַאֲרֻכִּים.
נָשְׁרוּ מִבִּינוֹנִיָּה, נָשְׁרוּ גַם הֵם. פֹּה שָׁם בְּלִי סִבָּה.

אַזְדֶּרֶכֶת מִתְחַתֶּוֶת אוֹהֶבֶת אֶת הַסְּתָו.
הֶחֱזִיקָה עוֹד יְמֵי שֶׁמֶשׁ. עוֹד עָלִים סְדוּקִים אֲרֻכִּים לְחוּדַיִים.
בְּלִי סִבָּה נָשְׁרוּ. נָשְׁרוּ גַם מִבִּינוֹנִיָּה בְּלִי רֹאשׁ.
עוֹד כַּמָּה יְמֵי שֶׁמֶשׁ. שַׁלֶּכֶת בִּנְשִׁיקָה. אוֹהֶבֶת הַסְּתָו.

Tree

Ask her if she remembers the summer — no.
Her evening is for nest snatchers from fear of shedding leaves
from rain sheaves of autumn
now.

The margosa tree is the night house of the shade. For the shade
is a house. An immigrant house for wild doves and other
summer wings. An immigrant house of wild bodies
and wild beasts ascend the tree. And now there is no one.

The violence of the rain from the autumn on the window.
Her lot fell. Sheds from her falls from her.
She can't. With bared arms got as far as the window.
The Yoreh is her death.

Leaves shed are like migrating birds.
In the winter shed and in the summer redress. But birds outside
and leaves within. And in the case before us leaves may also not return.
Believe it.

Who comes from the stars

Autumned margosa tree loves the autumn.
She has no crest and she has no quakes.
She held out a few more days. Leaves cracked and long.
Shed from begonia, they shed also. Here there without cause.

Autumned margosa tree loves the autumn.
She held out more days of sun. More cracked long separate leaves.
Without cause shed. Shed also from begonia without head.
A few more days of sun. Fall with a kiss. Loves the autumn.

אֵין בָּאָרֶץ עָלִים.
הִסְתַּוְּתָה מֵאֵלֶיהָ.
מָשָׁל עַצְמָהּ כְּלוֹמַר.
אָהַבְתִּיו אֶת הַסְּתָו.

קֵן בָּא וְקֵן הוֹלֵךְ. קֵן הָלַךְ מִן הַקַּיִץ. יָרַד בִּדְמָמָה לְעָנָף אַחֲרוֹן, כְּמֵת שֶׁמְּצָאוּ בַּדֶּרֶךְ.
אוֹתָהּ תּוֹר שֶׁנָּשְׂאָה חֵן, שֶׁבְּנָתָהּ אֶת הַקֵּן, נָפְלָה עָלָיו.
נוֹצָה אַחַת יָצְאָה לָהּ דֹּפֶן. יָמִים לְהִסְתּוֹבֵב
עִם הַסְּרָח. לְבַסּוֹף הַכֹּל הִתְיַשֵּׁר וְאוּלַי זוֹ יוֹנָה אַחֶרֶת. אוֹ לֹא.

הָיִיתִי רוֹצָה לִרְאוֹת תַּפּוּחִים עַל הָאֲזַדְרֶכֶת
שֶׁאֵין לָהּ תַּפּוּחִים. כַּמָּה כְּבָר זֶה זְמַן.
עַל הָעֵצִים יוֹשְׁבוֹת יוֹנֵי בָּר בְּיוּנִי
מְקוֹנְנוֹת אֶת הַמַּאֲדִים, מִי שֶׁבָּא בְּדֶצֶמְבֶּר.

אִם אֲפִלּוּ אַתְּ רַק עֵץ וְלֹא יוֹתֵר,
בְּשֻׁתָּף עִם אָדָם זֶה יַעֲבֹר לָךְ.
יוֹנֵי בָּר בְּרָמָה לֹא שׁוֹמְעִים אֶתְכֶן בַּחֹרֶף.
עַד תָּפְחוּ עֲנָפִים אַחֲרֵי חֹרֶף.

No leaves in the land.
They autumned off her.
By her self that is.
I have loved the autumn.

Nest comes and nest goes. Nest went from summer. Descended in
    silence to a last branch, like deadman found on the way.
Same turtledove that found favor, that built the nest, fell upon it.
One feather was out of her ordinary. Days to go round
with the stench. In the end it all straightened out and perhaps it's
    another dove. Or not.

I'd like to see apples on the margosa tree
that has no apples. How much already is it time.
On the trees sit wild doves in June
nesting the stew, who comes in December.

If even you're just a tree and no more,
in cooperation with man you'll get over it.
Wild doves on the height don't hear you in winter.
Till branches swelled after winter.

הגג חיוור מן העולם

הַבָּתִּים שֶׁבַּבַּיִת גָּרִים בַּדִּירוֹת.
אֲבָל הַגַּג גָּר בָּעוֹלָם וְחִוֵּר מִן הָעוֹלָם.
אֶת הַדִּירוֹת רוֹאִים הַבָּתִּים,
אֶת הַגַּג לֹא רוֹאִים אוֹתוֹ.

דּוֹמֶה כָּרוּחוֹת בְּסִינַי אַבּוּ זְנֵימָה,
הַמְפַסְּלוֹת גְּבָעוֹת וּפוֹסְלוֹת גְּבָעוֹת.
וְהַבָּא אֶל הַמִּדְבָּר לֹא יָבִין זֹאת.
לֹא יָבִין כִּי פָּסוּל הוּא.

כִּי הִנֵּה כַּבֶּטֶן שֶׁל אִשָּׁה.
אַחֲרֵי הַלֵּדוֹת לֹא לְגַשֶּׁת.
אֲדֹנָי אֲדֹנָי עוֹמֵד עַל צֵאת חַמָּה.
וְהוּא מְכֻסֶּה בְּלִי וִכּוּחִים.

וּבְאוֹתוֹ זְמַן עַל חֶבֶל הָרוּחוֹת מָסַרְתִּי כְּבִיסָה
קְטַנָּה כַּחֲבַצֶּלֶת שֶׁל חֶלִּית הַקְּטַנָּה.
וּבְאוֹתוֹ זְמַן אִשָּׁה וְרַגְלֶיהָ חֲלוּקוֹת
בְּחָלוּק רָאִיתִי מִן הַגַּג

הַר חֶרְמוֹן מִצַּד רָמַת הַגּוֹלָן זֶה הַר
חֶרְמוֹן אַחֵר. לוּחַ עֲנָק מֵאֶבֶן שַׁחַם כְּמוֹתוֹ
רָאִיתִי לְמַעְלָה עַל גַּג אֲרוֹן הַקֹּדֶשׁ בַּעֲיָרָה
אַחַת. אַךְ שָׁם זֶה הַרְבֵּה יוֹתֵר קָטָן וּמֵעֵץ.

שָׁמַעְתִּי מַכִּים אֶת הַבַּיִת.
לְהוֹרִיד אֶת הַגַּג בְּכֹחַ.
לְהָרִים קֶרֶן מַצָּה עַל מַכָּה.
וַאֲנִי גָּר תַּחַת הַגַּג.

מִבְנֶה הָרֵי זֶה מַמָּשׁ קַיָּם.
גָּרִים בּוֹ נַעַר וְזָקֵן.

THE ROOF IS PALE FROM THE WORLD

The houses at home live in apartments.
But the roof lives in the world and is pale from the world.
The apartments the houses see,
the roof they don't see it.

It's like the winds in Sinai Abu Zenaimeh,
that sculpt hills and cancel hills.
And the desert comer won't understand this.
Won't understand because he's canceled.

For it's like the belly of a woman.
After the births don't approach.
Adonai Adonai attends the coming of her heat.
And He covers without arguments.

And at the same time on the rope of the winds I put out the wash
little as the lily of little Helith.
And at the same time a woman and her legs divided
in a robe I saw from the roof

Mount Hermon from the Golan Heights side is another
Mount Hermon. A giant slab from granite rock like it
I saw on top on the roof of the Holy Ark in one
town. But there it's much smaller and of wood.

I heard they beat the house.
To bring down the roof by force.
To lift sledge-hammer blow after blow.
And I live under the roof.

A structure exists in substance.
Boy and old man live in it.

בַּיִת הֲרֵי זֶה מַשֶּׁהוּ קָשׁוּר בְּכֹחַ הַמְּשִׁיכָה.
תָּחַבְתִּי אֶת הַיָּד מִתַּחְתָּיו וּלְהָרִים לֹא יָכֹלְתִּי.

בַּיִת הֲרֵי זֶה חַי עִם כֻּלָּם טוֹב.
כֶּלֶב רָץ מֵאֵיזֶה חָרוֹן.
מֵאֵיזוֹ צְלִיפוּת, מֵאֵיזֶה עֶלְבּוֹן, בָּא
אֶל הַקִּיר, מֵרִיחַ חַיִּים עַל הַקִּיר, וָחַי.

הִנֵּה בַּיִת בְּקִרְבָתוֹ אֲנִי חַי.
בִּנְיָן עָגֹל כִּגְלָמִים שֶׁל הַצַּנָּה.
צוּרָתוֹ מִשְׁתַּנֵּית מִשִּׁפּוּךְ לְשִׁפּוּךְ.
וְהַיָּרֵחַ עוֹבֵר שָׁפוּךְ כֻּלְּבָנָה.

לֹא יִהְיֶה לְךָ לַעֲלוֹת אֶל הַגַּג.
לְשָׁם אֵין עוֹלִים יוֹתֵר.
שְׁנֵה כִּוּוּן יָמִינָה, שְׁנֵה כִּוּוּן שְׂמֹאלָה.
לֹא יִהְיֶה לְךָ.

זִיּוּפָךְ חוֹל וּמֶלֶט הֵם חָמְרֵי בִּנְיָן.
הָאֵשׁ וְהָעֵצִים וְהַמַּאֲכֶלֶת הֵם חָמְרֵי בִּנְיָן שֶׁל אַבְרָהָם אָבִינוּ.
זִיּוּפָךְ חוֹל וּמֶלֶט הֵם חָמְרֵי בִּנְיָן.
בַּעֲבוֹדָה שְׁחֹרָה כְּפוֹעֵל פָּשׁוּט שֶׁעָבַדְתִּי בְּבִנְיָן.

וַאֲנִי תַּעֲרֹבֶת טֶרֶם עָשִׂיתִי.
זֶה יוֹם עֲבוֹדָה שֶׁלִּי הָרִאשׁוֹן.
עָבַדְתִּי בְּבִנְיָן בִּימֵי הָאֵשׁ וְהָעֵצִים,
וּבָעֶרֶב חָזַרְתִּי עִם יְרֵכַיִם שְׁבוּרוֹת.

הֱבִיאוּ פּוֹעֲלִים מֵאִמְלַפַּחַם.
שָׂכָר שָׁוֶה בְּעַד עֲבוֹדָה שָׁוָה לִיהוּדִי וְלַעֲרָבִי.
מִפּוֹעֵל יְהוּדִי אֵין רֶוַח. אַךְ הַקַּבְּלָן בָּטוּחַ בְּרֶוַח.
מֵאַחְוַת עַמִּים שֶׁלִּי יֵשׁ רֶוַח.

A house is something bound by the power of attraction.
I shoved the hand under it and lift it I couldn't.

A house is alive if all are well.
A dog runs from some anger.
From some whipping, from some insult, comes
to the wall, smells life on the wall, and lives.

Here is the house in whose proximity I live.
A building round like the embryos of a play.
Its shape changes from renovation to renovation.
And the moon undergoes renovation as Luna.

You won't need to climb to the roof.
Nobody climbs up there anymore.
Veer right, veer left.
You won't need to.

Gravel sand and cement are building materials.
The fire and the trees and the knife are building materials of Abraham
    our father.
Gravel sand and cement are building materials.
At common labor as an unskilled worker that I worked in building.

And I a mixture still hadn't made.
It's my first day of work.
I worked in building in days of the fire and the trees,
and in the evening returned with broken hips.

They brought workers from Umilfach'm.
Equal wage for equal work for Jew and for Arab.
From a Jewish worker no rake-off. But the contractor is sure of a
    rake-off.
From my brotherhood-among-nations there's rake-off.

כָּאן יֵשׁ קַבְּלָן עוֹלֶה לִי עַל הָרֹאשׁ.
יַעַר "לַייסְטִים" וּ"קְרָשִׁים"-סָמוֹכוֹת הַצִּיג, הַצְּלָלִים הֵם הָעֵצִים.
גַּג עַל גַּג יָצִיק. כָּל חַיַּי לְהָצִיק.
וּמַה זֶּה כְּבָר אֲנִי גָּר פֹּה.

בַּלַּיְלָה, בְּגֶמֶר הָעֲבוֹדָה, הַגַּג חוֹרֵק כְּמֵאַשְׁפָּז.
צְעָדִים עַל הַמַּדְרֵגוֹת, בְּהַפְסָקוֹת, וְאֵין אִישׁ.
בַּלַּיְלָה צְעָדִים. וְכָל הַכֵּלִים עוֹנִים.
זֶה אוֹמֵר לִי: יֵשׁ לְךָ עִנְיָן אֶחָד: גַּג.

אֶת הַגַּג עַכְשָׁו סוֹגְרִים.
הוּא יִהְיֶה הַמִּכְסֶה שֶׁלִּי.
הַקַּרְנָס מְנַפֵּץ אֶת רֹאשׁוֹ.
מֵעוֹדִי לֹא שָׁמַעְתִּי קוֹלוֹ שֶׁל הַגַּג.

אִלּוּ שָׁמַעְתִּי אֶת קוֹלוֹ.
אִלּוּ עָמַדְתִּי קָרוֹב אֵלָיו.
קוֹלוֹ הָיָה מְדַבֵּר אֵלַי.
עַכְשָׁו שֶׁהוּא מִתְרַחֵק

שׁוֹמְעִים שֶׁהוּא מְדַבֵּר אֶל עַצְמוֹ.
עַכְשָׁו שֶׁנּוֹפֵל הַטִּיחַ, שׁוֹמְעִים שֶׁהוּא מְדַבֵּר אֵלַי.
הַגַּג מְדַבֵּר וְהַקַּרְנָס מַכֶּה אֶת הַגַּג.
וַאֲנִי שׁוֹמֵעַ יוֹשֵׁב בְּתַחְתִּית הַגַּג.

אֲנִי בֵּינִי וְהַתִּקְרָה.
אֲנִי בֵּינִי וְהַקִּירוֹת.
אֲנִי בֵּינִי וְהָרִצְפָּה.
אֲנִי בֵּינִי וְהַקִּיר וְהַמִּקְרָה.

בָּאֲלָטוֹת יָצִיקוּ בַּלָּאטְלָט.
בַּלַּיְלָה צְעָדִים דָּבִיק דָּבִיק.
בַּלַּיְלָה מֵרַעַם מִתְפַּשֵּׁט
מִן הַגַּג עַד מַרְתֵּף.

Here there's a contractor weighs me on the head.
A forest of moldings and 2 × 4 props points to, the shadows are the trees.
Roof upon roof he'll pour out. All my life to pour out.
And how's it already I live here.

At night, at the end of work, the roof rattles like an inmate.
Footsteps on the stairs, at intervals, and no one.
At night footsteps, and all the tools reply.
It says to me: you have one business: roof.

The roof they now close.
It will be my cover.
The sledge-hammer smashes its head.
Never have I heard the roof's voice.

If I had heard its voice.
If I had stood close-by it.
Its voice would have spoken to me.
Now that it moves away

you hear that it speaks to itself.
Now that the plaster falls, you hear that it speaks to me.
The roof speaks and the sledge-hammer beats the roof.
And I hear sitting in the nether roof.

I'm between me and the ceiling.
I'm between me and the walls.
I'm between me and the floor.
I'm between me and the wall and the incident.

Floor tile they lay clandestinely.
At night footsteps sticky sticky.
At night thunderfuse spreads
from the roof to basement.

אַתֶּם יְכוֹלִים לַעֲלוֹת עַל כָּל כּוֹכָב
וְתִרְאוּ פָּשׁוּט זֶה אֶחָד מִן הַבְּטוֹנִים
שֶׁנִּשְׁאֲרוּ מִן הַיְצִיקָה כְּפִי שֶׁאָנוּ מַכִּירִים
זֶה אַלְפֵי שָׁנָה אֲתַר הִיסְטוֹרִי.

חַיָּיו הָאֲפֹרִים שֶׁל כּוֹכָב.
יַקְרִינֻהוּ שָׁבִיט צַלַּקְתּוֹ הַוּוּלְקָנִית
בְּלֶהָבָה שֶׁל כִּירַיִם. בְּלִי לְהוֹדִיעַ עַל כָּךְ
יֵעָלֵם בְּחֹשֶׁךְ חֹשֶׁךְ.

חַיָּיו הַפּוֹרְשִׁים שֶׁל הַגַּג.
מִמֶּנּוּ רָאִיתִי אֶת הַכּוֹכָב וְאֶת הַשָּׁבִיט.
הַמִּשְׁפָּחוֹת בַּבָּתִּים שֶׁבַּבַּיִת.
וְהוּא לְבַדּוֹ נוֹתָר מִן הַיְצִיקָה.

הוֹפְכִים אֶת הַגַּג לָרִצְפָּה.
בָּאֲלֻטּוֹת יָשִׂימוּ חֲלַקְלַק.
רֶגֶל בָּהֶן עֲקֻמָּה.
יַבָּלוֹת עַל אֶצְבְּעוֹת הָרֶגֶל.

יְכַסִּימוֹ כְּמַיִם צוֹלְלִים.
זֶה הַגַּג יִהְיֶה הַמִּכְסֶה שֶׁלִּי.
וְזֶה יָבוֹא מִכֹּחַ הַמְּשִׁיכָה.
עַד שֶׁיָּבוֹא שָׁבִיט.

You can climb on every star
and you'll see simply it's one of the concretes
left-over from the pouring as we well know
it's thousands of years an historical site.

The gray life of a star.
A comet will radiate its volcanic
scar in the flame of a cooking stove. Without prior notice
will disappear in darkness darkness.

The dissident life of a roof.
From it I saw the star and the comet.
The families in the houses that are at home.
And it all alone it remained from the pouring.

You change the roof to a floor.
Floor tile put down all sleek.
Crooked foot thumb.
Corns on the toes.

It will cover 'em as water divers.
This roof will be my covering.
And this will come by power of attraction.
Until the comet comes.

אחרימן

אַחֲרִימָן. אַחֲרִימָן. מִסְתּוֹבֵב לִי בָּרֹאשׁ
הַשֵּׁם הַזֶּה כַּמָּה יָמִים וַאֲנִי
יָכוֹל לְהִזָּכֵר אֵיפֹה רָאִיתִי
אֶת הַשֵּׁם הַנּוֹרָא הַזֶּה.

מַה פֵּרוּשׁ הַדָּבָר? חִפַּשְׂתִּיו
בֵּין תְּפִלּוֹת
רֹאשׁ הַשָּׁנָה וְיוֹם הַכִּפּוּר,
מָקוֹם שָׁם מִתְגַּזֵּר דִּין

חַיִּים וָמָוֶת. בֵּין הַשֵּׁמוֹת
הַקַּבָּלִיִּים דְּקַרְנוֹסָא הַמְמֻנֶּה עַל
הַפַּרְנָסָה. הַמַּלְאָךְ הַגָּדוֹל
פַּצְפַּצְיָה וְהַמַּלְאָךְ הַגָּדוֹל

תָּשְׁבַּשׁ. מַדְעָן גָּדוֹל אֵינֶנִּי.
פַּעַם פַּעֲמַיִם תְּפִלָּה בְּצִבּוּר.
אֲנִי נִתְקָל בְּשֵׁמוֹת אֵלֶּה.
רַק אֶחָד אַחֲרִימָן אֵינֶנִּי מוֹצֵא.

וּמֵאַחַר שֶׁאֵינֶנִּי מוֹצֵא, עָשִׂיתִי לִי
מִלּוֹן מִמִּלָּה אַחַת. מֻכְרָח לִהְיוֹת
אִישׁ שֶׁמְּמַהֲרִים אֶת עַצְמוֹ. וְכָךְ אָמַרְתִּי:
אַחֲרִימָן – אִישׁ שֶׁמְּמַהֲרִים אֶת עַצְמוֹ.

אִם אוֹמֵר לְךָ מַשֶּׁהוּ יוֹם לְלַיְלָה,
זֶה אַהֲבָה.
אִם אוֹמֵר לְךָ מַשֶּׁהוּ לַיְלָה לְלַיְלָה,
זֶה אַהֲבָה.

יָמִים רַבִּים אָדָם אוֹהֵב. אוֹהֵב.
אִם אָמַר יוֹם וָלַיְלָה
זֶה אֵינֶנּוּ כּוֹזֵב.
לִהְיוֹת בּוֹר זֶה אוֹהֵב. בְּהַרְדָּמָה וִיקִיצָה זֶה אוֹהֵב.

וְהַיּוֹם, אִם שָׁנָה יִחְיֶה הָאָדָם
וְאִם אֶלֶף שָׁנִים יִחְיֶה,

Acriman

Acriman. Acriman. Goes round in my head
this name several days and I cannot
recall where I saw
this terrible name.

What does it mean? I searched for it
among the Rosh
Hashanah and Yom Kippur prayers,
the place where is decreed sentence

of life and death. Among the Cabbalistic
names Dikarnossa custodian of
livelihood. The great angel
Pitzpatzya and the great angel

Tashbash. A great scholar I'm not.
Once or twice prayer in public.
I come across these names.
Just one Acriman I do not find.

And since I do not find, I made me
a dictionary of one word. There must be
a man who incriminates himself. And so I said:
Acriman—a man who incriminates himself.

If I tell you something day to night,
it's love.
If I tell you something night to night,
it's love.

Many days a man loves. Loves.
If I say day and night
it's not lies.
To be a boor's to love. In dropping off and wakening it's to love.

And today, if a year a man lives
or if a thousand years he lives,

הוּא עוֹשֶׂה מִמֶּנִּי שִׂיחָה בְּכָל פֶּה.
וּמֵאָז אֲנִי לֹא בָּא עַל פָּנָיו.

יָכֹלְתִּי לָבוֹא. הָיָה מָקוֹם בִּשְׁבִיל הַיָּדַיִם:
הַיָּדַיִם בַּכִּיסִים שֶׁל הַמִּכְנָסַיִם
מִתַּחַת לַשֻּׁלְיוֹן שֶׁל הַזַּ'קֶט.
רְאֵה עֲמִידָה שֶׁל גְּבָרִים.

אֲבָל הוּא רוֹצֶה שֶׁלֹּא אֶהְיֶה.
וְגַם אֲנִי רוֹצֶה שֶׁלֹּא אֶהְיֶה.
אַף עַל פִּי שֶׁאֲנִי רוֹצֶה מְאֹד שֶׁאֶהְיֶה.
הוּא מַחֲרִים אוֹתִי, וַאֲנִי מַחֲרִים אוֹתִי.

וּבְשָׁעָה זוֹ עוֹד לֹא מָצָאתִי
בְּסִפְרֵי הַיְשָׁנִים וּבְסִפְרֵי הֶחֲדָשִׁים
אֶת הַמִּלָּה אַחֲרִימָן.
וְעוֹד אֵינֶנִּי יוֹדֵעַ מַה פֵּרוּשׁוֹ.

עָנִי וְאֶבְיוֹן הָיָה בָּא אֶל הַיַּיִן. הֵרִים בִּתְפִלָּה
לִפְנֵי הַמֶּלְצַר שְׁתֵּי אֶצְבָּעוֹת בִּקְצֵה גָּבַהּ
שֶׁל כּוֹסִית. הַמֶּלְצַר הֵבִין וְהֵבִיא.
פָּשַׁט הֶעָנִי וְקִבֵּל. הֵרִים הֶעָנִי וְשִׁבַּח וְשָׁפַךְ.

בָּא עָנִי אֶל הַיַּיִן כַּצֵּל וִדּוּי עַל הַקִּיר.
אַךְ הוּא עַצְמוֹ יוֹשֵׁב בַּחוֹמָה. וְאַחַת
לְשִׁבְעִים יוֹצֵא לִקְנוֹת נֵר
וּלְבַקֵּשׁ נְפָרוּר מִן הָעוֹבְרִים וְהַשָּׁבִים.

סָבוּר כִּי מְבַקְּשִׁים מִן הַיַּיִן
לֹא מִי שֶׁצְּרוֹר כַּסְפּוֹ כִּיסוֹ,
אֶלָּא מִתְפַּלֵּל בּוֹרֵא נְפָשׁוֹת
רַבּוֹת חֶסְרוֹנוֹת.

הוּא בָּא אֶל הַיַּיִן וְאָמַר:
אַתָּה מִתְנַשֵּׂא לַמֶּלֶךְ?
אוֹי שׁוֹשַׁנָּה שׁוֹשַׁנָּה שׁוֹשַׁנָּה שׁוֹשַׁנָּה.
צֵא מִן הַשֻּׁלְחָן.

he makes of me a colloquy on every lip.
And since then I keep away.

I could have come. There was place for the hands:
the hands in the pockets of the pants
under the slash in the jacket.
Observe: a stance of men.

But he wants me not to be.
And I too want not to be.
Even though I want a lot to be.
He incriminates me, and I incriminate me.

And for the present I still haven't found
in my old books and in my new books
the word Acriman.
And I still don't know what it means.

Poor as a mouse he'd come to the wine. Raised in prayer
before the waiter two fingers at the marginal height
of a small glass. The waiter saw and brought.
Stretched the poorman and got. Raised the poorman and praised and
    poured.

Comes a poorman to the wine like confession's shadow on the wall.
But he himself sits in the city wall. And one
in seventy goes out to buy a candle.
and ask a match of a passerby.

Assumes he asks from the wine
not one whose nest egg's his pocket,
but prays Creator of souls
full of deficiencies.

He came to the wine and said:
You lord it to rule?
Oh rose rose rose.
Leave the table.

הוּא בָּא אֶל הַיַּיִן לַמֶּלֶךְ:
אִם תֹּאמַר מִלָּה אַחַת
אֲנִי אֹמַר מִלָּה אַחֶרֶת.
חִצִּים נִתָּזִים אִם אָמַר.

הוּא בָּא וְאָמַר:
צֵא מִן הָאוּלָם.
אַתָּה אֵינְךָ מוֹדֶה.
אַתָּה תְּסֻבַּל מִזֶּה.

וַאֲנִי לֹא סוֹבֵל
וְלֹא שׁוֹבֵל.
אָז לָמָה אָמַר?
לֹא אָמַר

אֶלָּא כְּמַלְכֹּדֶת:
לְאַחַר חֲקִירָה קְצָרָה
הֵם מִסְתּוֹבְבִים מִפָּנַי.
כְּבָר לֹא נָעִים לִי.

הוֹשִׁיטוּ רֶגֶל וְעָבְרוּ אֶת הַבִּצָּה.
שֶׁטַח פָּתוּחַ.
אִישׁ, יָשֵׁן עִם עֲרִיסָתוֹ, הוּרַד לִקְרַאת קַרְקַע.
שִׁבְעִים שָׁנָה. אֶלֶף שָׁנִים, מַה זֶּה מְשַׁנֶּה.

פַּעַם לְשִׁבְעִים מֵת אַחֲרֵימָן.
לֹא יָכֹלְתִּי לְהָרִים אֶת הָעֵינַיִם.
נוֹשְׂאֵי הַסֵּבֶל לֹא רָצוּ לְהַבִּיט עָלַי:
הִנֵּה לֹא הֶחֱרִים אוֹתְךָ. הֶחֱרִים אֶת עַצְמוֹ.

עֵינַי זָרְקוּ בּוּשָׁה וְאַשְׁמָה. לֹא הָיָה מָקוֹם לְאוֹפְּטִימִיּוּת.

He came to the wine to rule:
If you say one word
I'll say another word.
Arrow spray if I say.

He came and said:
Leave the hall.
You don't plead guilty.
You'll suffer for this.

And I do not suffer
and do not shuffer.
So why did he say it?
He did not say it

except as a trap:
after a brief interrogation
they ambulate away.
It's already not pleasant.

They held out a foot and crossed the mire.
Open country.
Man, asleep with his cradle, is lowered toward land.
Seventy years. A thousand years, what does it matter.

Once in seventy Acriman dies.
I could not raise the eyes.
The train-bearers did not want to look at me:
for he did not incriminate you. He incriminated himself:

My eyes flung shame and blame. There was no room for optimism.

מי בא

גִּבְעוֹל קְטַן הַטֶּבַע.
צֶמַח מִצִּמְחֵי הַצִּבְעוֹנִים.
בּוֹדֵד כָּאֶצְבַּע עָלֶה בּוֹדֵד.
עָלֶה נוֹשֵׁר כְּפַרְפָּר.

מְרִיבַת צִפֳּרִים כְּמִשְׂחַק יְלָדִים.
יְלָדִים מְשַׂחֲקִים עַל הַחַיִּים וְעַל הַמָּוֶת.
מִכָּאן הַשְׁלָכָה עַל הַשַּׁלֶּכֶת
שֶׁחַיָּב בָּהּ הַגִּבְעוֹל הַקָּטָן.

הֶעָלֶה הַבּוֹדֵד נָשַׁר אֶל הָאָנָן.
בְּאַדְמַת יְלָדִים אֵינֶנּוּ.
עָלֶה יָרֹק. קֶבֶר יָרֹק. מִי בָּא?
מִי שֶׁבָּא לְקַחְתּוֹ תָּמִים.

Who comes

Nature's small stem.
A plant of the colored plants.
Lonely as a lonely leaf finger.
A leaf drops off like a butterfly.

Bird squabble like children's play.
Children play for life and for death.
From here a throwback to the fall
which imputes the small stem.

The lonely leaf dropped to the basin.
In children's ground it isn't.
Green leaf. Green grave. Who comes?
He who comes was duped.

עוד מוקדם

בַּלַּיְלָה יֵשׁ כַּמָּה דְּבָרִים שֶׁאֵינֶנִּי
יָכוֹל לְהִסְתַּדֵּר אִתָּם. בֵּינֵיהֶם
שֶׁהָלַכְתִּי לִישֹׁן מֻקְדָּם. וְעַד
אוֹר הַבֹּקֶר הָלַכְתִּי מֻקְדָּם.

חָשַׁבְתִּי לַעֲבֹר אֶת הָעִיר. הַגֶּשֶׁם
הַזֶּה שֶׁמְּצַפִּים לוֹ בָּאָרֶץ בִּדְמָמָה
קְפוּאָה, קָם מִלְּמַטָּה לְמַעְלָה לְאַט
וּפִתְאֹם. מֵהַגַּב נִשְׁפָּךְ, וְנִשְׁבָּר.

עוֹד מֻקְדָּם, עוֹד תְּחִלַּת סֶפְּטֶמְבֶּר. הָעֵץ
עוֹד יָרֹק. יוֹנַת הַבָּר עוֹד בָּאָה בָּעֶרֶב
מֵהָרָחוֹב מִלְבֶּשֶׁת אֲדַמְדַּם אֵשׁ חֲשָׁאִית.
וּבְבוֹאָהּ אֶל הָעֵץ מְרִימָה אֶת הַחִצּוֹנִית.

אוּלַי

תֵּלֵךְ הַיּוֹנָה אַחֲרַי.
שְׁתֵּי בֵּיצִים בְּבִטְנָהּ.
אֵלֶּה הַשְּׁנִיָּה הַקַּיִץ.

זְקִיפַת זְנָבָהּ מֵעָנָף לְעָנָף.
הַכְּנִיסָה הַמִּיסְטִית. הַנֶּעֱלָמוֹת בַּחֲשַׁאי.
בְּסִתָּן חַם. קִיר עָלִים.
מוֹלֶדֶת. אֶפְשָׁר לְהִשָּׁעֵן עִם הַגַּב.

עוֹד מְעַט תִּהְיֶה שַׁלֶּכֶת. וְהָעֵץ
פָּרוּעַ מֵעָלִים. יוֹנֵי בַּר נוֹדְדוֹת
וָאַיִן. עוֹד הַשַּׁלֶּכֶת לֹא
מֵהַיּוֹם לְמָחָר. אַךְ הָאָזְדָּרֶכֶת זוֹכֶרֶת.

Still early

At night there are several things I can-
not accept. Among them
that I went to bed early. And until
the morning light I went early.

I thought of crossing the city. This
rain which is anticipated in the land in frozen
silence, rose from down to up slowly
and suddenly. From the back it spilled, and broke.

Still early, still prefix September. The tree
still green. The wild dove still comes in the evening
from the street dressed in suspicious fire red.
And coming to the tree raises the skirt.

                          Maybe
the dove will follow me.
Two eggs in her belly.
Those her achievements this summer.

Her tail's verticular from branch to branch.
The mystic entrance. The disappearance in secrecy.
Hot little orchard. Wall of leaves.
Homeland. You can lean with the back.

Soon it will be fall. And the tree
bare of leaves. Wild doves migrate
and are not. While the fall is not
from today to tomorrow. But the margosa tree remembers.

מדינה מנגינה

אֲנִי סוּס אֶחָד. אוֹכֵל מִצַּלַּחַת אַחַת. כּוֹתֵב מִשַּׂרְווּל אֶחָד.
אֲבָל עִם חַבְרֵי קִבּוּץ עָבַדְתִּי בַּשָּׂדֶה.
הָיִיתִי מְקַנֵּא אֶחָד בַּפּוּדִינְג שֶׁהֵבִיאוּ.
הָיִיתִי רִאשׁוֹן בַּשּׁוּרָה.

כִּי הֵם עָבְדוּ בְּטוּרִיָּה־חֵצִי,
וַאֲנִי עָבַדְתִּי בְּטוּרִיָּה־שְׁלֹשֶׁת־רְבָעֵי.
פָּתַחְתִּי אֶת הָאֲדָמָה כְּאַפָּה שֶׁל פָּרָה.
כְּסוּס מֵרִים אַפּוֹ מֵהַמִּסְפּוֹא.

אוֹמְרִים לִי מִכָּל צַד: לְמִי יֵשׁ רֹאשׁ
עַכְשָׁו לְחַג הָעַצְמָאוּת תַּשְׁלַ"ד.
הַזְכִּרוּ־נָא הַזְכִּרוּ־נָא בַּטִּיּוּל,
הָרִאשׁוֹן לִיהוּדָה, וָאדִי קֶלְט, שְׁנַת פַּח.

עוֹד בַּיִת לֹא הָיָה לִי בַּבַּיִת.
סוּס בּוֹדֵד הָיִיתִי.
וּמִשָּׁם אִמִּי כּוֹתֶבֶת:
אֵיךְ אֲנִי יְכוֹלָה יוֹמְטִיב לַעֲשׂוֹת.

יָצָאתִי לְטִיּוּל. הָאָרֶץ מַזְמִינָה אוֹתִי
לְהִתְאָרֵחַ. אַף־עַל־פִּי שֶׁיָּדְעָה
כִּי מִן הַטִּיּוּל אֵין לִי לְאָן לָלֶכֶת.
אֲבָל זֶה רֶגַע חֲגִיגִי. אָז לָמָּה נַחְשֹׁב?

כִּי אִם אֵלֵךְ שׁוּנָה מֵאַיִן יָבוֹא לִי בַּיִת,
יְכוֹלָה הַגְּבֶרֶת לוֹמַר לִי: "אֲדוֹנִי,
זֶה כְּבָר לֹא". אָז כְּבָר הָלַכְתִּי וְסָחַבְתִּי מַיִם
מִמֵּימִיָּה אַחֶרֶת. וְלֹא הָלַכְתִּי לַקִּבּוּץ.

TUNE STATE

I'm one horse. Eat from one dish. Write from one sleeve.
But with kibbutz members I worked in the field.
I used to envy one the pudding they brought.
I was first in line.

Because they worked with a half-hoe,
and I worked with a three-quarter-hoe.
I opened the earth like a cow's muzzle.
Like a horse lifting his muzzle from the fodder.

From all sides they tell me: Who has a head
now for Independence holiday 5734.
But remember, but remember the hike,
the first to Judea. Wadi Kelt. Quick-pace on Pesach.

Still a house I didn't have at home.
A lone horse I was.
And from there my mother writes:
How can I hol-i-day make.

I set out on a hike. The land invites me
to be guest. Even though she knew
from the hike I have nowhere to go.
But it's a festive moment. So why think?

Because if I go other from where will I come by a house,
the lady could say to me: "My good man,
this already no." Then I had already gone and pinched water
from another canteen. And didn't go to kibbutz.

לָמָּה רָגְשׁוּ אוֹרוֹת שֶׁנִּשְׁקְפוּ מֵהַמַּיִם
שֶׁנִּשְׁאֲרוּ מֵהַגֶּשֶׁם שֶׁעָשָׂה אֶת הַשְּׁלוּלִית בְּ"דִיזֶנְגּוֹף סֶנְטֶר"?
יֵשׁ בָּהּ מָקוֹם גַּם לַיָּרֵחַ גַּם לִדְרִיסַת מַרְתֵּף
שָׁם מוּאֶרֶת: פַּסְצֵל. שֵׁדִים. חֲמָרִים. מוֹכְרֵי שְׂרוֹכֵי נַעֲלַיִם.

זֶה נִרְאָה עוֹלָם שֶׁהָיָה.
זֶה נִרְאוּ הַצְּרִיפִים שֶׁהָיוּ.
הַחַלּוֹנוֹת הַקְּטַנִּים בַּשְּׁלוּלִית.
הַצְּרִיפִים בְּצֶבַע בָּשָׂר וָדָם.

מִי מֵאִתָּנוּ לֹא הִתְפַּשֵּׁט מוּל הַכְּתָלִים
בֵּין הַקְּרָשִׁים הַשְּׁקוּפִים, הַקְּרָשִׁים?
מֵעֵץ לָבָן הוּא הַצְּרִיף וְהַשֶּׁמֶשׁ סָבִיב.
וּבִפְנִים הַדָּם. וּדְמוּת אָדָם.

בְּאַרְבָּעִים וּשְׁמוֹנֶה יָשַׁבְתִּי בַּמִּשְׁלָט.
כְּשֶׁיּוֹם יוֹם יוֹשְׁבִים זֶה הֶרְגֵּל לְאַט לְאַט.
הַמָּקוֹם הַשֶּׁפַע מֵהִשְׁשָׁבָה.
הַחֹמֶר הַטֶּבַע מֵהַיּוֹשֵׁב בְּמִכְנָסַיִם.

נָתַתִּי לוֹ אֶת מְעִילִי הָאָרֹךְ
לַחַיָּט שֶׁאֵינוֹ יוֹדֵעַ קוּנְצִים,
מַהֵר מַהֵר לְקַצֵּר
כִּי אֲנִי נוֹסֵעַ מַהֵר.

עָבַרְתִּי אֶת הַיָּם לְאַט.
יָרַדְתִּי בְּחֵיפָה. דּוֹקְטוֹר פְרַנְקוֹ מֵהַקְּרַנְטִין
שָׁלַח אוֹתִי מֵרְחוֹב לִרְחוֹב וּמֵרוֹפֵא לְרוֹפֵא.
וַאֲנִי הָלַכְתִּי לְקוֹצִים מִחוּץ לָעִיר.

אֲנִי (הוּא), הָעוֹלֶה הֶחָדָשׁ, (הוּא) עוֹד שָׁם?
בָּרוּךְ אֲנַדֶּרְתִּי עוֹד כָּאן?
בָּרוּךְ זֶה שֵׁם אָבִי.
אֲנַדֶּרְתִּי זֶה הוּא.

Why are the lights in an uproar that were reflected from the water
leftover from the rain that made the puddle in "Dizengoff Center"?
There's in it room also for the moon also for a basement flat
there lighted: Shadowline. Whitewashes. Clays. Shoelace sellers.

It looks like a world that was.
It looked like the shacks that were.
The little windows in the puddle.
The shacks the color of flesh and blood.

Who among us didn't strip against the walls
between the translucent boards, the boards?
Of white wood is the shack and the sun is about.
And inside the blood. And man's form.

In forty-eight I sat in the strong point.
When daily you sit it's a habit bit by bit.
The place was influenced by the sitting.
The clay was stamped by the sitter in trousers.

I gave him my long coat
the tailor who knows no flimflam,
swift swift to shorten
because I travel swift.

I crossed the sea slowly.
I disembarked at Haifa. Doctor Franco from the quarantine
sent me from street to street and from doctor to doctor.
And I went to the thorns outside the city.

I (him), the new immigrant, (him) still there?
Is Baruch my legend still here?
Baruch's my father's name.
My legend is him.

קַלּוּ הַמַּיִם בַּנָּהָר.
וְעַל הַקַּרְקַע נִרְאוּ דָגִים.
הוּחַסּוּ זְרָמִים וְגַלִּים.
וְשׁוֹמְעִים מַנְגִּינָה.

וְכָל עַמֵּי עֶרֶב
מַנְגִּינָתָם הָיִינוּ.
כִּי קַלּוּ הַגַּלִּים בַּנָּהָר.
וְהַמְּדִינָה מַנְגִּינָה.

בְּכָל דּוֹר וָדוֹר חַיָּב אָדָם
לִרְאוֹת עַצְמוֹ עוֹלֶה חָדָשׁ.
הִיא מְבַקֶּשֶׁת לְבַקֵּשׁ אֶת הָאֲדָמָה
וְלִשְׁתֹּק מִלְנַלּוֹת.

כְּשֶׁהָיִינוּ עוֹלִים הָיִינוּ מְאֻחָדִים.
כְּשֶׁהָיִינוּ בְּבֵית הַכְּנֶסֶת הָיִינוּ מְאֻחָדִים.
זֶה עַם לְכֻלָּם.
שְׁמַע יִשְׂרָאֵל, עַם אֶחָד.

The water subsided in the river.
And on the bottom fish were seen.
Muffled were currents and waves.
And a tune is heard.

And all the Arab nations
their tune we were.
Because the waves subsided in the river.
And the nation's a tune.

In every generation a man is obliged
to see himself a new immigrant.
It seeks to seek the earth
and not tell a soul.

When we were immigrants we were united.
When we were in the synagogue we were united.
It's a nation for all.
Hear O Israel, the Nation is One.

עד 15 מאי 1974

זֶה בְּדִיּוּק כְּחַדְרוֹן שֶׁחָדַר בְּסִתְוֹ וּמְחַכִּים בָּאָבִיב שֶׁיֵּצֵא,
וְלֹא יוֹדְעִים מָתַי יֵצֵא.
זֶה כְּמוֹ בַּבֹּקֶר קוֹרְאִים מוֹדָעַת אֵבֶל בָּעִתּוֹן וּמְחַפְּשִׂים שׁוּב לִרְאוֹת אֶת הַמּוֹדָעָה וְאֶת הַמָּקוֹם,
וְלֹא מוֹצְאִים אֶת הַמָּקוֹם.
אָבִי כָּל חַיָּיו עָבַד בְּטַחֲנוֹת קֶמַח.
עַכְשָׁו הוּא זֶרַע לָאֲדָמוֹת.

אֵין לִי אָח אֵין לִי רֵעַ. בַּדֹּחַף עָשִׂיתִי חֶשְׁבּוֹן לִמְצֹא אֶת הַקֶּשֶׁר כָּתוּב עִם כָּלַת
הַלַּיְלָה הָאַחֲרוֹנָה שֶׁמִּלְּלָה בַּעֲפַר הַסְקְרַייפֶּרִים בְּ"דִיזֶנְגּוֹף סֶנְטֶר". הַמְּנוֹפִים עוֹמְדִים
נְפוּחִים, אֶחָד אַחֲרֵי הַשֵּׁנִי. כְּמַחֲלָה מִן הַשָּׁמַיִם, תְּפוּשִׁים בַּשְּׁבָטִים. בְּמִצְלֵמָה לְמֵרָחוֹק, רֹאשָׁה
בַּשַּׁרְווּלִים. הַמְּנוֹפִים בְּ"דִיזֶנְגּוֹף סֶנְטֶר" עָבְרָה רוּחַ. הִתְעוֹרְרוּ
מִמַּשֶּׁהוּ דְּקָלִים עֲקֻמִּים. מְנוֹפִים.
הֵם אִידֵיאָל, הִנִּיחוּ צַוָּארָם עַל הָרְחוֹב. דְּקָלִים עֲקֻמִּים – עַמּוּדִים בְּכֹחַ –
הִנִּיחוּ צַוָּארָם עַל הָרוּחַ.
אֵין כְּכוֹכָבִים הַהוֹלְכִים לְאִבּוּד. כִּמְעַט לֹא הוֹלְכִים לְאִבּוּד.

כָּל חַיֶּיךָ הַכּוֹכָבִים
כָּל יָמֶיךָ הַלֵּילוֹת
עוֹמְדִים. בַּמָּקוֹם שֶׁעָמְדוּ.
וְהַמְּנוֹפִים כְּמוֹהֶם.

דְּקָלִים מִחוּץ לָעִיר יוֹתֵר חָפְשִׁיִּים. אֵינָם כֹּה זְקוּפִים וְחַיִּים בִּקְבוּצוֹת.
דּוֹמִים לִצְמָחִים מְאַשֶּׁר לְעֵצִים. לְיַד עַיִן מוּסָא
הַחַם, הַמַּעְיָן הַחַם בְּסִינַי הַחַם, יֵשׁ קְבוּצַת דְּקָלִים. עַל הַגִּבְעָה עַל הַמַּעְיָן עוֹמֶדֶת נָאקָה.
רָאֲתָה אוֹתִי, הִיא
הוֹלֶכֶת אֵלַי. רוֹאָה שֶׁאֵין לִי, הָלְכָה לִמְקוֹמָהּ.

UNTIL 15 MAY 1974

It's exactly like a lizard that penetrated in autumn and you wait in
   spring for him to come out,
and don't know when he'll come out.
It's like in the morning you read an obit in the newspaper and search
   again to see the obit and the place,
and don't find the place.
My father all his life worked in flour mills.
Now he is sown in earth.

No brother no friend. In the push I reckoned to find the connection
   written with the bride
of last night crushed in the dust of the scrapers in "Dizengoff Center."
   The cranes stand
swelled, one after the other. Like a sickness from heaven, held like
   comets. Like a camera from a distance, head
in the sleeves. The cranes in "Dizengoff Center" are inspired. Awakened
   from something were crooked palm trees. Cranes,
an ideal, they rested their necks on the street. Crooked palm trees —
   columns by force — rested their necks on the wind.
Nothing like stars for getting lost. Almost never get lost.

All your life the stars
all your days the nights
stand. In the place they stood.
And the cranes, like them.

Palm trees out of town are freer. They're not so straight and live in
   groups. More like plants than trees. Near hot
Ayun Mussa, the hot spring in hot Sinai, there is a group of palm trees.
   On the hill on the spring stands Naka. Saw me, she
walks up to me. Sees I have not, went her way.

אַנַא עַאיְשַׁה וַאַנַא מַאיְתַה
אֲנִי חַיָּה וַאֲנִי מֵתָה

הַאדַא שׁוּרוּל אַלְלַה
זֶה מַעֲשֵׂה אֱלֹהִים

אִז כַּאן בֵּית סַאוִּי הֵיךְ מַא בֵּית שׁוֹפְנִי אַבַּאדַאן
אִם תַּעֲשֶׂה כָּךְ לֹא תִּרְאֶה אוֹתִי בִּכְלָל.

אֱלֹהִים חָטַף אוֹתָהּ מִן הַחַלּוֹן
אָהַבְתִּי אוֹתָהּ מִן הַכָּבֵד שֶׁלִּי

לַגְּמַלִּים מֵעַיּוּן קַארָה, לְהַבְדִּיל עַיִּין מוּסַא, נָתַתִּי
לָהֶם לֶאֱכֹל גֶּדֶר צַבָּרִים קוֹצִים שֶׁל הַכֶּרֶם שֶׁשָּׁמַרְתִּי.
אַף־עַל־פִּי שֶׁהָיִיתִי שׁוֹמֵר וְהָיִיתִי מְצֻוֶּה עַל הַגָּדֵר לְבַל תֵּאָכֵל.
גְּמַלֵּי עַיּוּן קַארָה, רַבֵּי חוּט הַשִּׁדְרָה, אוֹכְלֵי הַקּוֹצִים,
אָכְלוּ אֶת סוּסֵי קְרָאסְנִיסְטָאוּו רַבֵּי הַמֵּרוֹץ וּמַקְצִיפֵי קֶצֶף לָבָן בֵּין הָרַגְלַיִם וְהַפְּחָדִים.
אָכְלוּ אֶת הַיְּלָדוֹת וְנִנּוֹחֶיהָ הַמְקֻפָּלִים, כַּעֲצֵי הַסְּקָה, כְּקָנֵי סֻכָּר.
אָכְלוּ אֶת עֲלִיַּת הַגַּג שֶׁל הַמַּהֲרַ״ל מִפְּרַאג.
אֶת ״סֵדֶר הַדּוֹרוֹת״. אֶת ״דִּבְרֵי יְמֵי עוֹלָם״. אֶת ״אָבוֹת דְּרַבִּי נָתָן״
שֶׁל סַבְתָּא שֶׁלִּי מֵעִיר מוֹלַדְתִּי נֶעֶסְבִּיזְשׁ.
אֶת הַחֶרֶסְתּוּמַטְיָה מִשְּׁנוֹת הָעֲשָׂרָה. אֶת הַגְּרַמַּטִיקָה הַלָּטִינִית מִשְּׁנוֹת הָעֲשָׂרָה.
אֶת אֲחוֹתִי הַקְּטַנָּה מִשְּׁנוֹת הָעֲשָׂרָה.
נָתַתִּי לָהֶם לֶאֱכֹל אֶת קְרָאסְנִיסְטָאוּו וְתֵל אָבִיב, בְּרִית עָרִים תְּאוֹמוֹת, בִּלְתִּי חֲתוּמוֹת.

Ana ayisha u'ana mayita
I live and I die

Hada shurul allah
It is God's doing

Iz kan bis sauyi haik ma bis shufni abadan
If you do that you won't see me at all

God snatched her from the window
I loved her more than my liver

For the camels of Ayun Kara, to differentiate Ayun Mussa,
I let
them eat the cacti thorns fence of the vineyard
I guarded.
Even though I was a watchman and I was charged with the fence lest
   it be eaten.
The camels of Ayun Kara, soft spinal corded, thorn
eaters,
ate the horses of Krasnystaw race masters and foamers of white foam
   between the legs
and doublefears.
Ate the childhood and its folded roofs, like firewood, like sugar
cane.
Ate the attic of the Maharal
of Prague.
The "Chronicles." The "History of the World." The "Fathers of Rabbi
   Nathan" of my grandmother from my birthplace
Neskhizsh.
The chrestomathy from the teens. The Latin grammar from the teens.
   My little sister from the
teens.
I let them eat Krasnystaw and Tel Aviv, pact of twin cities, un-
signed.

עַד כָּאן נָתַתִּי לָהֶם לֶאֱכֹל אֶת הַשָּׁנִים שֶׁהֶעֱלַמְתִּי אֶת הָאֱמֶת עַל מַצַּב הָאָרֶץ וּמַצָּבֵי הָאִישִׁי.
כָּל זֹאת אָכְלוּ כֶּאֱכֹל הָעִזִּים אֶת הָאֲרָזִים בָּאָרֶץ הַזֹּאת.
כָּל מַה שֶּׁשָּׁמַרְתִּי בְּגֶדֶר הַכֶּרֶם שֶׁשָּׁמַרְתִּי.
עַד עַכְשָׁו הַגַּמָּלִים לֹא אוֹמְרִים לִי כְּלוּם מִן הַכֶּרֶם שֶׁשָּׁמַרְתִּי.
עַד הָרֶגַע הָאַחֲרוֹן הַמְּנוֹפִים אֵינָם מְדַבְּרִים אֵלַי יוֹתֵר.
עַד חֲמִשָּׁה עָשָׂר מַאי הָיוּ יְלָדִים בְּצִפָּרְנַיִם צְפַרְדֵּעַ מְלַכְלֶכֶת.
מוֹרָשָׁה־בְּרֹשִׁיּוֹן צִפָּרְנַיִם אֲרֻכּוֹת מַמָּשִׁיּוֹת יְלָדִים שֶׁל קוֹרְצָ׳אק.

שָׁמַעְתִּי יֶלֶד אָבִים: "מִי יַעֲלֶה בַּמָּנוֹף?"
"אִישׁ אֶחָד וְצִפּוֹר" – אוֹמֵר הַיֶּלֶד.
"אַבָּא שֶׁלִּי שָׁכַח אוֹתִי" – אוֹמֵר הַיֶּלֶד.
"שַׁאֲלִי אוֹתִי עוֹד פַּעַם עַל אַבָּא שֶׁלִּי."

עַל דֶּרֶךְ עָפָר, בֵּין פַּרְדֵּס גּוֹלְדְבֶּרְג וְתֵל אָבִיב, עַל אֵם
הַדֶּרֶךְ, יָשְׁבָה אִשָּׁה בְּאֹהֶל קָטָן, עוֹשָׂה עֲדָשִׁים לְרַמַדָאן, אָמְרָה: "חוַאנְ׳ה,
לֵיל. חוַאנְ׳ה, הִגִּיעָה שְׁעַת לַיְלָה שֶׁל חֲשֵׁבוּת.
מִימִינִי תֵּל אָבִיב. יָפוֹ מִמּוּלִי, וּמִצְרַיִח "גַ׳מַע יֶפִי" אַחְמַד שַׁרַע מַכְרִיז פְּסוּקֵי רַמַדָאן.
וַאֲנִי הָלַכְתִּי בְּדֶרֶךְ הֶעָפָר וְחָשַׁבְתִּי עַל אֵם הַדֶּרֶךְ.

So far I let them eat the years I hid the truth about the country's
   condition and my personal
condition.
All this they ate as the goats eat the cedars in this
country.
Everything I guarded within the fence of the vineyard that
I guarded.
Until now the camels don't tell me anything from the vineyard that
I guarded.
Until the last minute the cranes don't speak to me
anymore.
Until the fifteenth of May children were in the fingernails of a dirty
frog.
From Warsaw-by-permit long fingernails serve children of
Korczak.

I heard child Avyam: "Who'll go up the crane?"
"One man and a bird" — says the child.
"My father forgot me" — says the child.
"Ask me again about my father."

On a dirt road, Between Goldberg Plantation and Tel Aviv, at
   cross-
roads, sat a woman in a small tent, makes lentils for Ramadan, said:
"*Chavadja*,"
eve. *Chavadja*, the night hour is come of
darkness.
To my right Tel Aviv, Jaffa opposite me, and from the minaret
   "Djama Yefi" Achmad Shara proclaims Ramadan
verses.
And I walked on the dirt road and thought about cross-
roads.

הַכְּבִישׁ שֶׁבֵּין שְׁנֵי חֶלְקֵי דִיזֶנְגּוֹף.
שֶׁהֵם שְׁנֵי חֶלְקֵי אֲדָמָה.
שֶׁהֵם שְׁנֵי אוֹקְאָנִים.
שֶׁהֵם שְׁנֵי מַיִם שֶׁהָיוּ.

וּשְׁנֵי הַצְּדָדִים הָיָה בּוֹ
מֵהַשֶּׁקֶט בְּמֶשֶׁךְ הַזְּמַן.
זֶה בֶּאֱמֶת כְּלוּם (הַמָּוֶת).
אָז אֵיךְ זֶה הִשְׁתַּקְּפוּ בַּשְּׁלוּלִית שֶׁהָיוּ?

פָּשַׁטְתִּי אֶת הַבַּיִת.
אֵיךְ לָבַשְׁתִּי בַּיִת?
עָזַבְתִּי אֶת אִמִּי.
אֵיךְ לָקַחְתִּי אִשָּׁה?

עָלִים אָזְנַיִם מְקֻפָּלוֹת.
מִישֶׁהוּ רוֹדֵף אֶת הָאַדֶּרֶת. אֵיזוֹ אֵשׁ.
רוּחַ אַחַת עֲנָפִים וּמְנַעֶרֶת
בְּיָדַיִם וּשְׂפָתַיִם קוֹלוֹת.

הָאַדֶּרֶת הִתְחִילָה בְּדִמְעָה.
שָׁמַיִם קַרְעֵי קַיִץ קַרְעֵי אֶרֶץ.
כְּנָפַיִם עוֹבְרוֹת מֵעָנָף לְעָנָף
סוֹד לְמָסְרָהּ.

טוֹב שֶׁלֹּא יוֹדְעִים עָלַי לְסַפֵּר.
הִתְחַלְתִּי מִבַּתְחִלָּה. מִבְּאֶמְצַע – כְּלוּם.
וְעַכְשָׁו אֲנִי שָׁב מִבַּסּוֹף. הֶחֱזַרְתִּי שָׁלוֹם
עַל אָמַרְתִּי שָׁלוֹם, כְּשֶׁנִּפְרַדְתִּי מֵאָבִי.

הָאֲנָשִׁים שֶׁחָשַׁבְתִּי יִהְיוּ קַיָּמִים בַּיָּמִים,
אֵינָם. אַתֶּם יְכוֹלִים לְתָאֵר לְעַצְמְכֶם.
כֹּל שֶׁכִּנָּה אוֹתִי בְּשֵׁם.
כֹּל שֶׁרָאִיתִי וְהִבַּטְתִּי – אֵין.

הַאִם אֱמֶת דִּבַּרְתִּי לְאָבִי: אֲנִי
הוֹלֵךְ לִבְנוֹת עִיר?
אוֹ זֹאת הָאֱמֶת שֶׁאָמַרְתִּי: "אֲנִי בּוֹרֵחַ
מִמְּךָ

The road that's between two parts of Dizengoff.
That are two parts of land.
That are two oceans.
That are two waters that were.

And the two sides it had
of the quiet in the course of time.
It is really nothing (death).
Then how is it they reflected in the puddle they were?

I took off the house.
How did I wear the house?
I left my mother.
How did I take a wife?

Leaves are folded ears.
Someone chases the margosa tree. What fire.
Wind gripped branches and shakes
with hands and lips voices.

The margosa tree began with a tear.
A sky summer tatters earth tatters.
Wings pass from branch to branch
a secret of transmission.

It's good they don't know about me to tell.
I started from the beginning. From the middle — nothing.
And now I return from the end. I returned goodbye
to my own goodbye on parting from my father.

The people I thought would exist in age,
aren't. You can well imagine.
Everything that called me by name.
Everything I saw and looked at — isn't.

Did I speak the truth to my father: I
go to build a city?
Or this the truth that I said: "I flee
from you

לְהַשְׁאִיר אוֹתְךָ לְלֹחֵךְ אוֹתְךָ
הָאֵשׁ וְהָאֲדָמָה". "יָבוֹא זְמַן
וּתְקַבֵּל סְטִירוֹת לֶחִי" – אַתָּה אוֹמֵר לִי בַּחֲלוֹם.
"וּמִי יָבוֹא לָתֵת לְךָ סְטִירוֹת לֶחִי" – אֲנִי עוֹנֶה לְךָ בַּחֲלוֹם.

מִמֶּנִּי וּמֵאָבִי
נִשְׁאָר אֲנִי.
נִשְׁאָר אֲנִי
לְהַגִּיד לְךָ.

הַיּוֹם הַהוּא וַאֲנִי עוֹמֵד עַל חוֹף חֵיפָה וְאֹכַל
וְלֹא יָדַעְתִּי מֵעֵץ הַקּוֹצִים הַקַּצְקְצַקִּים הַקְטַקְטִים הַסַּבְרִיִּים שֶׁחָדְרוּ
לְגוּפִי וְחָזוּ מִבְּשָׂרִי וְעָלוּ בְּיִצּוּעַי וְהִתְחַלְתִּי בְּפִנְקָס קָטָן
יוֹמָן יוֹם אֶחָד בְּאֶרֶץ-יִשְׂרָאֵל יוֹם שְׁנַיִם בְּאֶרֶץ-יִשְׂרָאֵל.

כָּל כָּךְ מַעֲשֵׂה בְּרֵאשִׁית בָּאתִי,
עַד שֶׁהָיִיתִי מַמְשִׁיךְ מַעֲשֵׂה בְרֵאשִׁית
וַיְחִי אָדָם וַיְחִי שֵׁת וַיְחִי אֱנוֹשׁ
כָּל בְּרִיאַת עוֹלָם שִׁבְעָה יָמִים.

שֶׁהֵם שִׁבְעָה יָמִים בַּשָּׁבוּעַ
שֶׁהֵם אַרְבָּעָה שָׁבוּעוֹת בַּחֹדֶשׁ
עַד לַחֳדָשִׁים עַד לְשָׁנִים
עַד לַעֲשָׂרוֹת שָׁנִים.

בֵּינְתַיִם אִבַּדְתִּי אֶת הַיּוֹמָן כְּמוֹ הַרְבֵּה דְּבָרִים
שֶׁהֵבֵאתִי מֵהַבַּיִת כְּמוֹ הַנְּאוּם שֶׁלִּי לִפְתִיחַת
הָאוּנִיבֶרְסִיטָה כְּמוֹ הַחֲלִיפוֹת שֶׁזָּרַקְתִּי מֵהֶם וְאַחַת
שְׁחֹרָה וַחֲגִיגִית מָסַרְתִּי לַנַּהָג וְלֹא הָלַכְתִּי לְקַבֵּל.

בְּרִיאַת כָּל הָעוֹלָם שִׁבְעָה יָמִים.
הֵם שִׁבְעָה יָמִים – וַאֲנִי אִבַּדְתִּי אֶת הַקֶּשֶׁר.
שָׁכַחְתִּי לִסְפֹּר. עָבְרוּ יָמִים, שְׁנַיִם,
שָׁנִים, שְׁנֵי שָׁנִים.

120

to leave you to devour you
the fire and the earth." "The time will come
you'll get your face slapped" — you tell me in the dream.
"And who'll come to slap your face" — I answer you in the dream.

From me and my father
remains me.
Remains me
to tell you.

That day and I stand on Haifa shore and eat
and did not know of the bramble-barbed minuscule prickly pear thorn
    tree that penetrated
my body and felt in my bones and climbed on my couch and I began
    in a small notebook
a diary of day one in Eretz Yisrael day two in Eretz Yisrael.

So genesiswise I came,
that I might have continued the genesis
and Adam lived and Sheth lived and Enosh lived
the whole world creation seven days.

That are seven days of the week
that are four weeks in the month
until months until years
until decades.

Meanwhile I lost the diary like a lot of things
I brought from home like my speech for the inauguration of
the university like the suits I threw out for the heat and one
black and ceremonial I gave to be pressed and didn't fetch.

The creation of the whole world seven days.
They are seven days — and I lost the connection.
I forgot to count. Days went by, changes,
years, two years.

וְהַשָּׁנִים עוֹשׂוֹת שַׂק אֱגוֹזִים.
אֵלֶּה שֶׁלְּמַעְלָה הַשַּׂק הֵם אֱגוֹזִים.
וְאֵלֶּה שֶׁלְּמַטָּה נִבָּטִים נִשְׁחָקִים נִשְׁכָּחִים
נִדְחָקִים נִדְקָרִים דּוֹחִים וְיוֹצְאִים מְהֵרִים בַּשַּׂק.

וְהַזְּמַן הַזֶּה כַּמָּה לֶחֶם סִפְּקוּנִי
וְכַמָּה מַיִם לִרְוָיָתִי וְשֶׁמֶשׁ
וְרָצוֹן טוֹב
מִן הֶעָבִים.

אֲבָל הָאֱגוֹזִים דִּלְמַעְלָה
וְהַנִּרְאִים לָעַיִן מִלְּמַטָּה מַבִּיטִים עָלַי
לְטוֹבָה. אַף כִּי
דַּי אֱגוֹזִים קָשִׁים.

וְאִם אֲנִי אוֹמֵר אֱגוֹזִים אֲנִי מִתְכַּוֵּן
לָאֲנָשִׁים שֶׁזּוֹכְרִים אוֹתִי בִּשְׁמִי הַקּוֹדֵם
עַד שֶׁמֵּתוּ. וַחֲבָל עַל דְּאָבְדִין
שֶׁלֹּא יָדְעוּ אֶת שְׁמִי הֶחָדָשׁ.

שְׁמִי הַקּוֹדֵם. מַה אֶעֱשֶׂה פֹּה בִּשְׁמִי
הַקּוֹדֵם. כָּל אֶחָד פֹּה בִּשְׁמוֹ הַקּוֹדֵם.
אִלּוּ פֹּה נוֹלַדְנוּ. עָשִׂיתִי בְּצַלְמִי כִּדְמוּתִי
יַד אַבְשָׁלוֹם שְׁמִי כָּל אֶחָד יוֹדֵעַ.

And the years make a sack of nuts.
Those at the top of the sack are nuts.
And those at the bottom ogled pounded forgotten
huddled punctured delaying and emerging from holes in the sack.

And that time how much bread it supplied me
and how much water to drink my fill and sun
and good will
from the clouds.

But the nuts on top
and that are visible from the bottom look at me
kindly. Even if
pretty tough nuts.

And if I say nuts I mean
people who remember me by my previous name
until they died. And woe for the lost ones
that didn't know my new name.

My previous name. What will I do here with my previous
name. Everyone here with his previous name.
Were we but embryo here. I made in my image after my likeness
Absalom's Hand is my name everyone knows.

Notes

POEM IN THREE

The collection
The last poem of the series, "Poem in Three." The order of the poems, arranged according to the date of their composition, should be: "The watch," "The lover," and "The collection." I have taken the liberty of opening with the last poem of the sequence.

The watch
l. 3: The Swiss, as a neutral nation of watchmakers, are conservative in their advertising copy; "a gray revolution," as opposed to the "red" of other revolutions.

ROCKET AND BIRD PLANT

Bird plant
l. 5: "Simchath Torah" (literally, "the joy of the Torah") is the holiday that marks the completion and initiation of the annual cycle of weekly synagogue readings from the Pentateuch. The "flag," carried by children, was traditionally also a receptacle—the flag stick was crowned with an apple which bore a lighted candle in place of a core.

POEMS AT HOME

The wild dove
The small, terra-cotta colored ringdove. These doves mate and nest on window sills and, although wild, are often familiars of the household.

Victim nest
l. 19: "Kinnereth," the Sea of Galilee; actually a lake into which the Jordan flows and emerges again with diminished strength.

A NOVEL WITHOUT CLOTHES

"I wanted to reach a small case"
ll. 49–50: The association of Yeshurun's townsmen is with *pustenish*, the Polish word for wasteland or desert, which sounds to them like "Palestini"—Palestine on Polish lips.

Friday, 24 Tammuz 5733, 27 July 1973
l. 18: "Phosphates." The phosphate industry, sponsored by the government, changed the face of the Dead Sea.

THE SYRIAN-AFRICAN RIFT

A geological formation that, on Israel's side, extends from the Huleh region, through Lake Kinnereth, down the Jordan Valley and the Dead Sea to Eilat and the Red Sea.

In "Letter #41 (broken off)" of the *Maximus Poems*, Charles Olson writes:

> ... The Jews
> are unique because they settled astride
> the East African rift. Nobody else will grant
> like he said the volcano anyone of us does
> sit upon, in quite such a tangible fashion.

The background of this group of six poems is the October or Yom Kippur War of 1973. The surprise attack found two-thirds of the nation in the synagogue. The major part of the call-up consisted in locating the particular synagogue of the reservist and pulling him out as quickly as possible without overly disrupting the prayer service.

The poem on this day
l. 12: A journalistic dilemma of christening. These two names competed in the communications during the early weeks of the war, the former eventually winning out.

The poem on the Africs
l. 2: "*Tallith*," the prayer shawl, usually worn in the synagogue; now seen in the streets, as soldiers already in uniform were pumped for information by the congregants. There are no newspapers or radio broadcasts on Yom Kippur in Israel.

The poem on our Mother Our Mother Rachel
l. 3: Biblical Jacob confuses the 1970s reservists with the late prime minister and his party secretary of the 50s.
l. 5: The late President Yitzchak Ben-Zvi had a knotty-pine annex to his house, which served as an official reception room. The furnishings were homely, true to the tenor of the state in the early years. Ben-Zvi, while president, was known to visit the Jerusalem cinema unaccompanied and on the spur of the moment.
l. 6: Batia Lishanski, a member of the Second Immigration wave; well-known sculptor.

Quadruple
l. 2: "Pita" is a flatbread of the Middle East.
l. 24: "The Canal," the Suez Canal.

We hear his river
A traditional elegy. Perhaps written after the death of the Hebrew poet Natan Alterman, whom Avoth Yeshurun admired.

PLEASE DON'T ASK

"I say hello"
l. 3: The poet whimsically uses the singular "glass." The impression is of sharp, bright slivers.

PACKAGES

The series title is hebraized Yiddish — *Pekla'oth*. The Yiddish *peklach* (bundles) is given the Hebrew plural ending. The poem has a prose epigraph (omitted) which closes, "... And when you destroy an old house, oi it's no good. Tel Aviv the holy city."

Poem from Tel Aviv
ll. 11–12: The 1930s of Avoth Yeshurun's Little Tel Aviv was also the period of a mass hebraizing of old names. The equivalent translations, often officially suggested by the Language Institute of the time, frequently retain the shadow of their original. Thus "Tapuchi," an adjectival form of the Hebrew word for apple, since "Eppelboim" (apple tree) would be ridiculous in Hebrew. To avoid confusion and facilitate the payment of debts, the old name was sometimes also kept.
l. 24: "The Wall" is the Western Wall, or "Wailing Wall," almost all that remains of the Second Temple.
ll. 37–38: "Mister Bialik...his primiparous way." The national poet, Chaim Nachman Bialik; like a woman who gives birth for the first time — Bialik's Hebrew.
l. 43: "Soilless clay" (*nazáz*), a technical term familiar to agriculturists, possibly from the Arabic. Nothing will grow in *nazáz* as roots will not pierce it.

Lullaby for Nordia Quarter
l. 3: "Ohel Shem," literally, "the tent of the Name." One of the early, active Tel Aviv theater groups, now defunct.
ll. 22–23: Yeshurun plays with historical terminology for the two Jerusalem Temples.
l. 25: "As Father bought." The phrase is from the most famous song of the Passover Haggadah, "*Chad Gadya*" ("One Kid"). The original source (in Aramaic) reads, "As Father bought with two *zuzim*."
l. 30: These are the "state" funerals, as it were, of the most illustrious names of the *Yishuv*, the Jewish community of pre-state Israel. Achad Ha-Am is the pseu-

donym of Asher Ginsberg, a most persuasive polemicist and master of a lucid Hebrew prose style that is a model to this day. His adopted name means "one of the people." Nordau's fame is firmer in the world of Zionism than of Hebrew letters.

THREE LITTLE-GIRL POEMS

Poem no. two
l. 2: "Gordon" is "Aleph Daled" Gordon, well-known for his ethic of a nation of workers. He advocated a return to simple values, to the soil, to a natural diet in order to make up for an interminable exile and the restrictions of a gray ghetto life, and to rebuild the nation on a sounder and more normal basis. Gordon was one of the key figures of the "Second Immigration," and the idol of many literary figures of the 1920s.

SEVEN ON THE RAIN

Three
ll. 2–3: "*Talleisim*," the Yiddish plural for prayer shawl. "Kol Nidrei," a prayer recited on the eve of Yom Kippur.

Four
ll. 7–8: "Dooba" is teddy bear. "Shamash," puzzlingly, is in the feminine. Whether or not the reference is to the Akkadian sun god, the bitch escapes the bad weather in the hope of some place warmer.

Seven
The poem takes off from a beautiful phrase in the High Holiday liturgy, *ha-dofkim bi-tshuvah*, "those who knock in repentance." But *dofek* in contemporary Hebrew slang is also the common verb for the sex act, equivalent to "screw" or "bang" in English. ll.7–8 bear consciousness of this.

January 1st, night
l. 6: "Habima" is the Hebrew National Theater.
l. 12: "I remember" is in English written in Hebrew characters. The translator gets no credit for the rhyme.

LOCAL POEMS

Growth
l. 2: "Development" is also in English written in Hebrew characters. The theory here, seemingly abstruse, is valid for poetry and experience as well as for music. Compare John Ashbery's lines from "The Skaters":

> ... Except to say that the carnivorous
> Way of these lines is to devour their own nature, leaving
> Nothing but a bitter impression of absence, which as we know
> involves presence, but still.

l. 16: Yeshurun equates his beloved Quarter with the famous Santa Caterina Monastery in Sinai, and Solomon's Temple.

End of summer
l. 17: "Psalms." The reference is to David's Book of Psalms. Yeshurun gives them the highest literary rating.
ll. 18–20: A paraphrase of the stunning, baroque *Akdamoth Milin*, an Aramaic composition that is recited on the festival of Shavuoth.
l. 52: "Desert Dead," the title of Bialik's famous long poem from the turn of the century, *Meitei Midbar*.

THE ROOF IS PALE FROM THE WORLD

"The houses at home..."
l. 14: "Helith" is the name of Yeshurun's daughter—who grew up to become, at one time, Israel's foremost fashion model, and the Hebrew translator of Samuel Beckett's *Molloy*.

"Gravel sand and cement..."
"Gravel" in the Hebrew is *zifzif*. It would have been worth preserving the word—almost as odd in Hebrew as it might have been in English.

TUNE STATE

"I'm one horse"
l. 10: "5734," the Hebrew calendar date, equivalent to 1974.
l. 12: "Wadi Kelt" is about twenty minutes from Jerusalem by car, on the road to Jericho. "Pesach" is Passover, the spring festival.

"Why are the lights in an uproar..."
l. 2: "Dizengoff Center," a huge building complex in Tel Aviv. It began snail-like because of the difficulty in removing shack-dwellers who, from earliest times,

squatted at the corner of Dizengoff and King George Streets. Like many such ambitious financial projects, it began with an enormous hole in the ground. The rented German cranes are five years active, and feel at home.

"In forty-eight..."
'48 is the magical formula for the Israel War of Independence. Everybody was somewhere in '48 and all local histories tend to revolve about the date. There is a generation of '48 poets and novelists, a repertoire of popular songs of '48, "the spirit of '48," and so on.

"The water subsided in the river"
l. 8: The sense of the line is the same as in the epigraph to John Berryman's *77 Dream Songs*, "... I am their Musick" (Lamentations 3:63).

UNTIL 15 MAY 1974

"For the camels of Ayun Kara"
l. 11: "Krasnystaw," the Polish town where the poet was brought up.

l. 34: "[Janusz] Korczak," the Polish Jewish writer and educator who refused to leave the orphans under his charge and was killed, together with them, by the Nazis.

"That day and I stand on Haifa shore and eat"
l. 40: "Absalom's Hand," *Yad Avshalom*, is the tomb that lies just outside the walls of the Old City of Jerusalem above the village of Silwan. The actual hand that once topped the dome is long gone. The facade of the structure is pock-marked with the stone-throws of Orthodox Jews. Absalom, as a paradigm of the disobedient son, is pummeled by the passerby by custom and present practice.

Avoth Yeshurun: A Chronology

September 9, 1904   Born Yechiel-Alter Perlmutter in Neskhyzh, a village in Volhynia in the western Ukraine. According to the Hebrew calendar, the date of his birth fell on Yom Kippur. His grandfather owned a water mill where his father worked. His mother was the daughter of the *Rebbe* of Neskhyzh. The family, whose Hasidic roots went back many generations, included three other sons and a daughter.

1909   The family moves to the town of Krasnystaw, where the five-year-old lad receives his first instruction in a traditional Yiddish *cheder*.

1914   With the outbreak of World War I, he returns to Neskhyzh with his mother. The father remains behind in Krasnystaw, but later rejoins the family. Together with other families from the village they wander, as part of a band of Jewish refugees, from town to town for a year.

1915   The family returns to Krasnystaw to find the city ravaged. The boy is privately tutored and grows up in the shadows cast by the distress of the war and amid severe economic suffering.

1917   First attempts to write poetry in Yiddish.

1918   The rise of an independent Poland, with its stirrings of hope, makes a strong impression on the adolescent youth.

1920–25   Reads extensively in world literature in Polish translation, as well as in Yiddish and Hebrew literature. The first Hebrew book that he read was a translation, by Kalman Shulman, of Eugène Sue's *Les Mystères de Paris*. Becomes one of the founders of Hebrew courses in Krasnystaw, and is drawn to the Zeirei Zion movement. Decides to emigrate to Palestine, despite the objections of his parents. His departure frees him from conscription into the Polish army.

October 14, 1925   Arrives in Palestine.

1926–29   During his first years in the Land of Israel he frequently changes his place of residence while searching for work. Lives in Tel Aviv, Magdiel, Kfar Saba, Raananah. Roams the country's Arab-Jewish villages working as a building-hand, watchman, swamp-dredger, and fruit-picker. During these years he also becomes attracted to the milieu of the East, its inhabitants, its way of life, and its customs. In addition, he is drawn to the Hebrew poetry of Uri Zvi Greenberg, especially

	the volume *Hagavrut ha'olah*. Greenberg is the poet closest to him in spirit. In 1926 he begins to compose his first poem, *"Tzom vetzima'on"* ("Fasting and Thirst"), which was not to be published for another eight years.
1929	Joins the Haganah, the major Jewish military force in the years preceding independence. Assumes a part in the defense of Jerusalem against the Arabs in Atarot.
1931–32	Works as a watchman in the vineyards around Rishon le-Tziyon. Deepens his familiarity with the Arab world.
1934	Marries Pesyah Justman, an education secretary active in the labor movement. His first poem, "Fasting and Thirst," is published in the journal *Turim*, a rallying-place for modernist writing.
1936–38	Experiences intensely the violent clashes with the Arabs during the years of the anti-Jewish riots in Mandatory Palestine. Is on active duty with the Haganah.
1939–45	1942 sees the birth of his only child, his daughter Helith, who will become a model, poet, and translator. In the same year he publishes his first book of poems, *Al chochmat derachim* (On the Wisdom of Roads), under his original name. During the years of World War II, all communication with his family in Poland is cut off. The family perished in the Holocaust.
1948	In Israel's War of Independence, serves in the infantry on the Syrian border, near the mouth of the Jordan, not far from Lake Tiberias. The war with the Arab states dashes the hopes he had long entertained for a life of shared experience with the Arabs. Changes his name to Avoth Yeshurun, meaning "the fathers are looking (at us)." Begins work on his cycle of poems *Tzevet utzevat* ("Team upon Team"), which address themselves to the Holocaust and connect that tragedy with the Arab problem.
1952	Publishes his poem *"Pesach al kuchim"* ("Passover on Caves") in the daily *Ha'aretz* (May 23, 1952). It arouses a controversy because of its nonconformist attitude regarding the Arab question. He responds with the poem *"Ruach be'arbe"* ("Wind in the Locust").
1955	Serves for a short time as a voluntary guard in Kibbutz Nachal Oz, on the border of the Gaza Strip. This experience echoes in several of his poems.
1961	Publication of his second volume of poems, *Re'em* (Thou Shalt Lead Them). All his time is now taken up with his literary work.
1964	Publication of his third volume of poems, *Shloshim amudim shel Avoth Yeshurun* (Thirty Pages of Avoth Yeshurun).
1967	Is awarded the Brenner Prize in Literature.

1970 Publication of his fourth book of poems, *Zeh shem hasefer* (This Is the Name of the Book). Becomes a regular contributor to the literary journal *Siman Kriyah* that began to appear at this time, and gains great esteem among the journal's other contributors, considered to be the new generation in Hebrew letters.

1974 Publication of his fifth book of poetry, *Hashever ha-Suri Afrikani* (The Syrian-African Rift), which includes poems written against the background of the Yom Kippur War.

1977 Publication of his sixth volume of poetry, *Kapella kolot* (A Chorus of Voices).

1979 Receives the Bialik Prize for Literature.

Prepared by David Weinfeld, Hebrew University

LIBRARY OF DAVIDSO